✔ KU-314-278

Introduction to finches and softbills

by Hank Bates & Bob Busenbark

By Henry Bates and Robert Busenbark

Photography: HARRY LACEY

Published by T.F.H. Publications, Inc., T.F.H. Building, 245 Cornelison Avenue, Jersey City, N. J. 07302. Distributed in the British Empire by T.F.H. Publications (London) Ltd., 13 Nutley Lane, Reigate, Surrey, England. In Canada by Clarke, Irwin & Company Ltd., Clarwin House, 791 St. Clair Avenue West, Toronto 10, Ontario, Canada. Printed in the U.S.A. by the lithograph process by T.F.H. Lithograph Corp., Jersey City, N. J. 07302.

Distributed to the Book Trade in the U.S.A. by Crown Publishers, Inc., 419 Park Avenue South, New York, N. Y. 10016.

Contents

The cover shows Cutthroat, or Ribbon, Finches
in full color.

Chapter I

INTRODUCTION

If you are just starting out with finches, you are in for some of the most rewarding experiences ever offered by any hobby. These tiny creatures with their myriad colors and interesting patterns have just as much variety in their fascinating personalities. The best way to enjoy them is to have a diversified collection so that you can enjoy the contrasts and similarities of their colorful community life.

Your first finch may possibly have been selected for a variety of reasons. You may have had an empty cage in which you wished to put "something different." Or you wanted a songbird a little out of the ordinary. If so, you probably bought a Green Singing or a Strawberry Finch. Perhaps you bought a pair of Zebra or Society Finches so that you could raise a little family within a cage. Maybe you just saw a pretty and unusual little bird with a low price tag.

Regardless of the reason, you have made the start. If you want to multiply your pleasures, you will not stop with just one bird or one pair. This book will guide you through the better selections of the various finches and will instruct you in proper diet and care so that you will be spared many errors.

Do not expect finches to learn to talk like a budgerigar or to sing like a cultured canary. If you demand performances in addition to rainbows of colors and a myriad of natural charms, you may be disappointed. If you are interested in a close relationship with the beauty and variety of kaleidoscopic nature, you will find just such an absorbing involvement with finches. Some finches have silvery little songs which crop up at unexpected moments; others spend most of their time rearing families; several undergo a complete change of color during the breeding season during which they give elaborate performances or displays to attract and to entertain mates; and some just offer beauty.

Finches are usually small birds ranging from three to six inches in length. They are mainly dependent upon seeds as the major source of their foods and are therefore called *hardbills* as opposed to *softbills* which live mainly upon soft fruits and insects. There are variations in diet, however; and some birds in this book are omnivorous in that they utilize many items in both basic diets.

For the most part, finches in a grand array of readily available species from all over the world are very inexpensive. Some are among the least costly birds in all of aviculture which is a term embracing the entire field of keeping birds in captivity. There are, of course, many rare and expensive finches for the advanced connoisseur; and there are even more in a medium price range.

Many people prefer to specialize with one family of finches. In such specialized studies, it is possible to delve much further into all the more subtle ramifications of bird keeping. One such interesting sideline specialization is the study of genetics in the rapidly mutating Zebra Finch. There are now many color varieties available in the pretty little Zebra Finch. By applying the principles of genetics, it is possible to develop many new varieties as further mutations occur.

Welcome to the hobby. The writers hope you will find complete enjoyment in your newfound avocation. As you progress and expand in this hobby you will doubtless be interested in further literature in this vast subject; and so we would like to recommend our larger and far more complete volume, *Finches and Softbilled Birds*, which is available at leading pet shops everywhere.

Chapter II

DIET

The simplest diet is most likely to be the most faithfully administered. Unfortunately, no one can group all the necessary ingredients into one feeder, but we can reduce the number of ingredients to a very few and still maintain maximum nutrition. The diet is the most important single factor in maintaining good health and long life.

The basic finch diet consists of finch mix, health grit, greens, a dietary supplement, an insectile mix, and cuttlebone. Some birds require certain modifications such as the addition of extra niger, extra canary seed, fruit, mealworms, and spray millet. Those who require these extras will be mentioned under their respective headings. Spray millet, while needed by some, is relished by all finches as a treat food.

Finch mix consists of four parts of small Australian millet, two parts of plain canary, one part white proso millet, and one half part oat groats. Some pet shops also include niger in their finch mixes, but the writers prefer to feed it in a separate dish if it is necessary. Canary treat or song food has niger and several other helpful seeds, some of which aid plumage.

Webby seed is not necessarily old or stale. A tiny seed moth becomes active during hot months and goes through its breeding cycle in bird seeds. Webs are from its little caterpillars. The birds do not object to the webs. In fact they derive added nourishment from the caterpillars. This moth, by the way, is not a clothes moth.

Dietary supplements are available in several selections. Liquid vitamins for birds can be added to drinking water with no fear of evaporation as is the case with liquid vitamins for humans. Powdered or ground supplements usually contain additional trace minerals necessary in a bird's diet. These can be added to seed mixes or, in several cases, fed in separate containers.

Cuttlebone provides necessary calcium and should be in every cage and aviary. The soft side should be accessible to the birds.

Health grit or gravel serves two purposes. It acts as a grinding agent for seeds in the bird's crop and, if it is a true health grit, adds necessary minerals. Some bird gravels contain too much charcoal which is helpful to birds only in very small amounts.

Green food should be given to birds every day instead of the occasional or sporadic feedings given by some people. When given at intermittent intervals, greens may cause diarrhea because the birds overeat when they are given such opportunities. Fresh greens should be washed to remove harmful residue from insecticides. Yellow or pale greens do not contain sufficient nutrition. Rich nourishing green food always has a dark green color. Examples are carrot tops, dandelion, water cress, and spinach. Lettuce and celery are low in food value for birds.

Red Headed Finches in family grouping. From left to right, female, two fledgings, and an adult male. Note that the adult female lacks the red head of the male.

Dehydrated greens are now available on the bird market. These are very simple to feed because they may be mixed with seeds or supplements.

Live foods are necessary for several finches on a year-round basis and for many others at breeding time. Mealworms are the most easily obtainable live food and may be found at pet shops. They are extremely nourishing, but they usually should be rationed because they may be too rich. An average of two to three per day is sufficient for most finches, but this amount can be doubled or even tripled during the breeding season.

Mealworms can be raised at home in a simple culture of red bran with a little raw apple or carrot to provide needed moisture. The entire breeding cycle takes about six months. Mealworms are the larvae of beetles which do not fly and which live their entire life within the red bran medium.

Mockingbird food or softbill meal is also helpful in supplying the insectivorous requirement of many finches. Many birds will ignore this fare, but some take to it quite readily and frequently arouse the interest of other birds as well. Oily mockingbird food should be avoided because of its indigestibility.

Apples and, to a lesser extent, oranges are very nourishing to finches. The writers limit oranges because of their high acid content and feed only red apples, avoiding green apples completely.

Chapter III

AVIARIES, EQUIPMENT, AND BREEDING

AVIARIES

Though many finches are bought with the idea that they are to be caged birds, these birds usually do much better in aviaries. Collections of vari-colored birds and breeding accommodations are more easily possible in aviaries. Cages are all right for many birds, and a few species will even rear families in them. Large cages are adequate for small collections of congenial birds, and the close intimacy between birds and owner in such cages is an interesting experience. For the smaller birds, finch spacing is necessary because some of the tiny waxbills fly right through some of the wider cage bar spacings. Pet shops usually can supply a wide range of sizes and designs in cages to fill all tastes.

Aviaries must be built to fit individual tastes and situations. If the aviary is to be built within a house or under the wide overhanging eaves to be found on patios or lanais, then there is no need for an additional shelter. If it is a garden aviary, it should consist of an open, wired flight, an enclosed shelter, and a safety door.

A safety door is an enclosed or wired vestibule-like area between two doors. This prevents escapes. If a bird escapes from the aviary, it can easily be retrieved from the intervening area.

The extent to which a shelter must be enclosed will depend upon weather conditions during the winter. In really mild climates, three sides and a roof are necessary only to provide cover during inclement weather. Aviaries in cold climates usually have larger shelters than the ones in mild climates because it may be necessary to enclose the birds within a shelter for considerable periods during bad weather. For enclosed shelters, small access doors between flight and shelter may be constructed so that they may be closed up to keep the birds inside the shelter during storms.

The population of any aviary should not be crowded. Overcrowding brings about many problems including easy transmission of contagious diseases and personality adjustments in which certain individuals may become bullies.

Location of the aviary depends upon prevailing wind factors. The shelter must also be a shield against wind because drafts are extremely hazardous.

Construction materials may run the full gamut in personal preferences. Frameworks for flights need not require heavy duty timbers unless the flight is to be of a really large size. Some aviaries have galvanized metal pipe frameworks. These are ideal in appearance and require a minimum of upkeep. In most cases, two by two inch lumber is satisfactory. Over this aviary mesh will be laid. Either one-half inch diameter hexagonal aviary netting or one-half by one inch welded wire fabric is satisfactory. The aviary netting is cheaper, but it requires a lot more stretching if it is to remain taut. If the wire is painted black, its view obstruction will be held to a minimum.

Floors may be of concrete, soil, or turf. Each has its advantages. Concrete is more expensive but is easier to maintain and clean. Turf is pleasant in appearance but requires some upkeep. Soil is not widely used because it must be frequently turned to remove accumulated filth which can become dangerous. Moreover, unless solid foundations on all sides of the aviary run into the ground for eighteen inches, mice, rats, and snakes may gain easy access into aviaries which have soil floors. All these pests are especially dangerous to birds.

In addition to gaining access through a soil floor, these predators may enter aviaries at ground level through the wire mesh. This can be prevented in most cases by adding a metal shield rising two feet high all around the outside of the open flight.

There are other predators from which the birds must be protected. Neighborhood house cats are the source of many injuries at night when the birds are frightened off roosts and dash headlong into walls of wood or wire. The birds cannot see at night, but the cats can. A double roof about eighteen inches above the wire netting will remove the worst danger from these nighttime panics. Moreover, if the upper roof is very flexible or resilient, the cats will not tread upon it because they will be unable to gain a firm footing. In some cases surplus wartime camouflage netting has been useful for this upper roof.

Planted aviaries are very attractive and are wonderful for many birds. Chances for breeding several of the shyer species are greatly improved in planted aviaries. Large populations of some birds and even small collections of weavers may result in continual defoliation; so it is wise to select both plants and birds accordingly if you wish to bring the garden inside your aviary.

Some very satisfactory plants and shrubs for aviaries are olive trees, bottle bushes, pittosporums, privets, *Euonymous*, *Forsythia*, *Cotoneasters*, the Tulip Tree or deciduous magnolia, honeysuckle, small bamboos, and even *Pyracantha*. Poisonous plants such as oleander and castor bean should, of course, be excluded.

Multiple flights are ideal for large and diversified collections and are necessary for extensive breeding operations. Wherever multiple flights are used, servicing the aviaries is greatly simplified by expanding the safety door into a safety aisle. This, in addition to preventing escapes, also makes it unnecessary to enter any but the desired flight. If food and water receptacles can be arranged on pull-out trays or serviced through small doors in the safety aisle, the birds do not undergo any disturbance.

AVIARY EQUIPMENT

Equipment for aviaries consists of perches, waterers, baths, feeders, and nests. In cold climates a heating arrangement may also be necessary. Feeders in many variations are available at pet shops. Some of the many wild bird feeders are especially attractive as well as useful. Select as many as will be necessary to supply the different foods you will be offering.

Waterers also are available in different styles at pet shops. You may select a shallow open dish or a bath for wild birds which will double as a bathing facility as well as a waterer. Or you may prefer one of the gravity type waterers which keeps water cleaner and which is especially recommended if you wish to include liquid vitamins in drinking water. Birds quickly learn to use most gravity waterers; but until they do learn, place open water dishes just beneath all gravity waterers.

Perches should fit the feet of the birds to be housed in your aviary. Small twiggy branches are excellent, but they should be replaced frequently since

A pair of Cutthroat Finches. The male on the left can be recognized by the gash (red) across the throat. Females are less boldy patterned throughout.

they are difficult to keep clean. Hardwood dowels are neat, easily installed, and are easily scraped clean with a perch cleaner.

Different birds prefer different types of nests. Most finches prefer covered boxes or wicker nests. Some like canary nests, and some should be offered both so they will make their own choice. It is very wise to have more nests than there are pairs of birds so selections will not involve stalemated disagreements. Miniature doves nest well in Yorkshire Canary nests.

Heating arrangements, wherever necessary, should be installed with primary regard to safety for the birds. Some forms of heating may emit gas fumes to which birds are particularly sensitive. Electricity is safest, but in some areas it is expensive. The most efficient and inexpensive electric heating device is cable heating. Electric cables which mildly exude warmth can be placed in strategic areas throughout the aviary where birds will congregate to receive the benefit of the warmth. Of course, power may fail during storms. No heating arrangement is completely foolproof, but cable heating remains free from most hazards. If expense is no object, a series of pipes through which hot water passes may be laid in concrete flooring.

A night light should be a standard fixture in all aviaries and should be placed over food supplies. If any disturbance during the night frightens a bird from its perch, it will gravitate to safety near such a light. Also, any sick bird will seek the warmth from such a light and will be easily detected. Otherwise it may huddle in some obscure corner and may escape the attention of the bird fancier.

BREEDING

Supplies for the nests include nest pad linings for the canary nests and nesting hair, both of which are obtainable at your pet shop. In addition, quantities of dried grasses will be needed for nesting material. You can obtain these grasses from any clean unfouled area in your garden. Dry them out for a few days and place in an easily accessible hopper. Many people fashion a hammock from unused aviary mesh to keep the grass up off the floor. Frequent restocking of nesting material may be necessary throughout the breeding season.

Nestling food serves as a good conditioner just prior to the breeding period. Most people prefer to feed it dry up until two days before the first eggs hatch and then moistened throughout the rest of the breeding season.

Incubation for most finches lasts from twelve to fourteen days. Youngsters may remain in the nests for varying periods with different species. On an average, however, it runs between two to four weeks at the most. Youngsters are weaned after they leave the nest, and this too will vary according to species.

As a rule, the parents start to work on another clutch of eggs right away. An average pair raise two nests per year, with three to four youngsters per nest. Doves have only two eggs and usually rear both youngsters. Overbreeding weakens parents and offspring alike. It is difficult to stop Zebras and Societies from breeding unless the nests are removed.

To leave nests in an aviary for the entire year is wrong. They become infested with mites and are badly soiled. Remove and clean them up at the end of the breeding season.

Breeding seasons differ according to native origin. Most finches change their breeding periods to our spring, but Australian finches are usually stubborn and often adhere to the fall despite several generations of aviary breeding in this country. Zebra and Society Finches breed at any time of the year. They are so thoroughly domesticated that they would actually prefer to be nesting all the time.

Variations from these schedules and necessary dietary additions will be detailed under coverage for the birds.

Chapter IV

DISEASES AND AILMENTS

As with most birds, clearing up diseases and ailments in finches is not an easy task; but, if the principles in Chapter II regarding diet and sensible care are followed, prevention is simple. Many birds may fall prey to many diseases and ailments, but finches actually acquire very few disorders. There are some disorders from which birds do not recover, but most of these are so easily avoided that preventive measures are just good common sense.

The most important aspect of any illness is the recognition of the first signs of danger because few illnesses in their last stages ever result in a satisfactory recovery. Loss of stamina and the will to live occur remarkably fast, and all diseases show rapid inroads upon stamina.

Average symptoms for most illnesses include listlessness, lack of sheen on plumage, lusterless eyes, puffy feathers, and, in most cases, loose droppings. A quick loss of weight indicates the rapidity with which the ailment takes hold.

FIRST AID

Very often the only necessary treatment to bring about a miraculous recovery for a sick bird is immediate First Aid. Basic components of first aid are heat (approximately 80 degrees Fahrenheit, constant day and night), appetizers, generous and easily accessible food supplies, and a precautionary antibiotic to ward off secondary infections.

To apply heat to any cage, cover the cage on three sides and the top and place a twenty-five-watt light bulb either on the inside or close to the outside of the remaining open side. Do not worry about a loss of sleep. If the bird should awaken it will be encouraged to eat, and this gives a very positive chance for recovery. Without heat most birds show no interest in food. Life is always at its lowest ebb during the night, and the addition of heat at night helps to prevent that life from slipping away.

The cage should be prepared for first aid by removing all except one very low perch and by placing food and water in open, easily accessible dishes. Liquid appetizers are now available on the market to add to the drinking water. These very often help appreciably in reducing the downward trend by stimulating an interest in food.

USEFUL MEDICATIONS

Available at most pet stores are certain medications which every bird fancier should always have on hand to meet emergencies.

There are two antibiotics in the form of bird remedies obtainable at pet shops. The most efficient for most illnesses and the one used first by the writers is a liquid containing sulfamethazine. The second is aureomycin which is available in pill form to be dissolved in water. Both these remedies may be used together. Follow directions carefully.

Antibiotics are frequently overused by bird fanciers because they are usually the first to be recommended. Overuse sometimes causes liver and kidney problems and digestive upsets because desirable and helpful bacteria are killed along with the detrimental ones.

Liquid appetizers are invaluable, but they unfortunately are not yet well distributed. The basic components of most appetizers are Vitamins B1 and B12.

Yellow oxide of mercury (ophthalmic style) in a two percent strength helps most eye conditions and even assists in opening clogged sinuses in some cases.

Two blood coagulants may be used for birds: hydrogen peroxide in a household strength and iron sulfate (popularly called Monsel's Salts). Since birds cannot afford much loss of blood, immediate coagulation of any bleeding wound is necessary. After bleeding, all dietary supplements assume greater importance to help restore losses.

ENTERITIS

Infectious enteritis is perhaps the most deadly and most frequent of all illnesses encountered by birds. It is caused by overcrowded and dirty environments during acclimation. Complete isolation, first aid, and sulfamethazine are the most effective treatment.

GOING LIGHT

Going Light is a rapid loss of weight. It is an old term used too frequently because it is a symptom and not a disease. Look for other causes before making a diagnosis.

DIGESTIVE UPSETS

Digestive upsets may result in constipation, diarrhea, and sour crop. Sour and impacted crops may be relieved by a simple treatment which consists of dissolving one teaspoon of baking soda into a quart of distilled water. Use this solution in place of drinking water for two days. Symptoms and treatment for both diarrhea and constipation may be very similar. Both conditions cause loose droppings, and both may be indications of other disorders. A simple treatment consists of one tablespoon of black strap molasses mixed into a pint of distilled water. This laxative clears up the digestive tract enabling it to function properly and also offers quick, easily absorbed food value. This solution should be used instead of drinking water for two or three days if a careful examination fails to disclose other ailments.

RESPIRATORY DISORDERS

A cold is the simplest and first form of respiratory disorders. It should be treated quickly and effectively to prevent further dangerous infections or complications such as asthma, impacted sinuses, and pneumonia. Colds are caused by drafts and exposure to temperature extremes. The writers instigate first aid and add both aureomycin and sulfamethazine according to instructions on packages. Moreover, one of the more effective cold remedies and an inhalant prepared especially for birds is administered to speed recovery. Pneumonia is treated the same way. Impacted sinuses may result from backlogged mucus which cannot drain properly during untreated colds. Nostrils must be uncapped and cold remedy and inhalant administered.

The most discouraging aftermath of a cold is asthma which is difficult and time consuming in treatment. Cures may not be realized even for treatments up to six months. Heavy, labored breathing and audible rasps are indications of asthma. Treatment consists of constant first aid and an occasional administration of an antibiotic. A decongestant cold remedy and a bird inhalant should be given every day.

FOOT DISORDERS

In addition to overgrown toenails, the only other problem affecting feet is bumblefoot. This painful disorder can be traced to improper circulation caused by poor diet and lack of exercise. The swollen feet show lumpy cheeselike deposits under the skin. Too oily a mockingbird food and too many mealworms are also frequent causes. A good blood builder will help the circulatory system in carrying off these deposits if they are not already extensive. If surgery becomes necessary, it should not be extensive, so that shock and heart failure may be avoided. A small incision cut lengthwise into the nodule and gentle pressure will permit the removal of the substance. If bleeding occurs, apply a blood coagulant and an astringent.

OVERGROWN BEAK AND TOENAILS

Overgrown beaks are rare in finches unless a deformity is present. Clip back to the normal length as often as is necessary. Certain species of finches, notably Strawberry Finches and Nuns, are bothered by chronically overgrown toenails which are hazardous because they become entangled in aviary mesh. Frequent clipping may be necessary. Leave the toenails slightly longer than the normal length to avoid cutting into the veins. If bleeding should occur, apply hydrogen peroxide or iron sulfate for coagulation.

BROKEN BONES

Broken bones knit very rapidly in birds, and usually a week's recuperation will clear up all debility from a broken leg. Treatment, though simple, is not always dependable in outcome. Broken wings are not so easily overcome because they sometimes knit imperfectly resulting in a deformity which might affect flying ability.

Enforced disuse is the best treatment for broken bones. The hospital cage should be small with only one perch placed near the floor and food and drinking water placed within easy reach. The writers also administer first aid to overcome shock. Birds aid in this treatment by favoring the broken limb.

EGG BINDING

Inadequate exercise and improper diet may bring about egg binding which uses up all the bird's strength in a very short time. Treatment to be effective must be immediate. Symptoms involve frequent straining attempts to expel the egg, weakness, and puffed feathers. Often the egg can be felt in a bulge above the vent. First aid plus a mild, warm household oil inserted into the vent usually are successful in ejecting the egg.

Softshelled eggs are the result of inadequate mineral supplements, especially calcium. Birds which have suffered from either of these problems should not be allowed to nest again for at least six months.

MITES

Though many mites and lice affect birds, the red mite is the only one which is widespread. Red mites cluster in corners and crevices during the day and creep out at night to feast upon bird blood. They become most active during hot summer months. Weekly sprayings during these periods may be necessary to control mites. Some of the various aerosol sprays at pet shops do not require removal of birds or foods and are the easiest to use. Pyrethrins are the safest of all mite killers, but they are slower than most.

FEATHER DISORDERS

Two feather problems occasionally afflict finches. One is feather plucking, which is an acquired bad habit, and the other is melanism, which is an odd discoloration of feather pigment. A regular late summer six weeks molt is not an ailment but a natural occurrence to replace old feathers. Canary molting food with its increased animal protein factor is advisable during the molt. Liquid vitamins or powdered vitamin mineral supplements may be added to foods.

Too much heat or too much sunshine through glass may cause out of season molts. This usually happens to caged birds rather than to aviary birds. Relocating the cage usually corrects the cause.

Feather plucking is an insidious habit which is difficult to eradicate once it becomes entrenched. Sometimes it is caused by one bully and sometimes it is a practice showing widespread participation brought about by overcrowding. Some species are prone to feather plucking. Among these especially are the Green Avadavat, Cuban Melodious, the Lavender, and to a lesser extent, various waxbills. Affected individuals should be isolated until all feathers have been replaced. This seems to be the most effective device for quelling such habits.

Melanism is an odd but harmless disorder resulting in a dark brown shade overpowering all normal coloring. The health is not affected; but the condition should be corrected by proper diet, natural sunshine, and an ample supply of fresh greens.

Chapter V

AUSTRALIAN FINCHES
AND PARROT FINCHES

Several of the loveliest and most ideal of all finches in aviculture come from Australia. Unfortunately, all except Zebra Finches are becoming increasingly scarce. An export ban at present prohibits any more of these lovely birds from being sent out of Australia. Zebras are very prolific and so are very plentiful and inexpensive. Star Finches are becoming steadily more domesticated. Prices are coming down, and production is up. Lady Goulds are imported regularly from Japan, and many are produced in the United States, but there are some difficulties which will be explained during the coverage of the species.

The rest of Australia's beautiful finches are difficult to get, and prices are getting higher all the time. This is an excellent branch for specialization by bird fanciers who wish to raise birds. Some of the brightest gems in the bird world need not become the rarest.

With proper housing and diet, a majority of Australian finches are surprisingly successful in breeding aviaries. Unfortunately, most bird breeders are not putting forth enough effort in this direction even though demand is always high.

All except four of Australia's finches are Grassfinches. Three are Mannikins, and one is a Waxbill, but they all will nevertheless be covered in this chapter.

The diet of all Australian Finches is simple and similar. The standard finch fare plus plentiful quantities of spray millet is adequate. Mealworms in small quantities are helpful if the birds will accept them, but an appetite for this food must be acquired. Those birds who do accept them usually do so because they imitate other birds who consume them readily. A dish of insectile mixture may be substituted instead of mealworms, but these finches must also learn to accept this food by imitation just as they do mealworms.

The breeding season of Australian birds is the opposite of ours starting in our fall. Zebras have bridged the gap and nest at any time. A few others have been progressively delayed until our spring, but the natural inclination is to start in October and November. Therefore, the bird fancier should provide protection and possibly heat if his birds breed at this period. Birds improperly nourished or inadequately exercised are prone to egg binding during cold weather.

Most Australian finches nest in the standard finch nest box but it is also wise to offer the open canary nest to several species in case they prefer it. Eggs hatch in about twelve days, and young leave the nest between two and three weeks of age.

ZEBRA FINCHES

The most abundant of all domesticated finches is the pretty and easily reared Zebra Finch. He can be found in several different color varieties. The original or wild variety is the very inexpensive Gray Zebra Finch. All of the other color variations were brought about during breeding in captivity. Since all are the

A pair of Red Headed Gouldians. The hen (at left) is quite young. The cock is about two years old.

same species, they interbreed freely. All are prolific, but new varieties may be slow becoming abundantly established.

The Gray Zebra Finch is about four inches long including its tail of one and one-fourth inches. The upperparts are gray and underparts are mostly dusty-white with some significant and colorful accents on the male. The beak is bright orange-red on the male and paler orange on the female. Feet and legs are orange in both sexes.

The male is very attractive with its large cheek patch of bright rust-red and its broad chestnut area on the sides and flanks. The chestnut area is spangled with small white spots. The chest and chin have very fine zebra bars of black and white. The female lacks these markings.

Both sexes have bold black and white bands on the tail, and small black and white accents which resemble tear stains below the eyes. Youngsters resemble females until about three weeks after they leave the nest. During this time the beaks are grayish at first. The orange starts at the base of the beak and spreads gradually.

White Zebra Finches are beautiful in their gleaming whiteness. The only other color is the brightly contrasting orange on beaks, feet, and legs. Males have a darker shade of red-orange on their beaks and can therefore be easily distinguished from females. Some youngsters show flecks of gray and black on the tips of several flight feathers until they mature. White Zebras are only slightly more expensive than the Grays.

18

Silver Zebras are marked like Gray Zebras, but they have a pale silver-gray replacing the darker areas of the Gray Zebra. Usually the price is low on this color variety too.

Marked White or Chestnut Flanked Zebras are becoming more readily available all the time. This is a newer color variety which at first was relatively high in price. It still is considerably more costly than the White Zebra Finch. Marked Whites are like Silvers except all the gray areas are diluted to white. The other accents are present, but they are somewhat subdued. The male is very pretty because the orange cheek patch and chestnut sides are excellent contrasts. The female is just like the White Zebra except she has the black tear-stain accent marks below the eyes.

There are several other color varieties or mutations of Zebra Finches, but all are rather rare and costly in this country. They are highly interesting to specialists and students of genetics. If the reader becomes interested in any of these rarer varieties he will find more information and illustrations in *Finches and Softbilled Birds*.

LADY GOULD or GOULDIAN FINCH

No one can adequately describe the rather expensive and lovely Lady Gould. It is easily one of the most beautiful birds in the world. The purple chest and bright golden underparts dominate the color scheme, but the green upperparts are rich and smooth, and the finely drawn turquoise accents surrounding the eye and framing the face are particularly vivid. The size of the bird is about five inches long, including a long taper-tipped tail of one and one-fourth inches. The two central feathers have long, almost bare shafts for added elegance.

The female is similar but much subdued in coloring. The chest is especially dull by comparison.

The male Red Headed Lady Gould is even more beautiful than the black-faced variety. This subspecies occurs in the wild state in Australia, but it is not as prevalent as the black-faced variety. The only difference is a brilliant red velvet-like area superimposed over most of the facial area. Black is still present in a fine black frame across the top of the head and in a broad flaring area of the chin and throat.

The female Red Headed Gouldian is like the female Black Headed Lady Gould except that she has some red on the face. The red is variable in extent and intensity, but even traces of red on the face means she is of the red-headed variety.

The Yellow Headed Lady Gould has a dull, rather unattractive shade of rusty-orange in place of the red. It is not accurately named, nor is it as beautiful as either of the two varieties described. The dullness of the face is incongrous alongside the other brilliant colors. It is more rare, however, and the price is nearly always higher.

Experiences vary with the Lady Gould Finch. Many bird fanciers report excellent breeding success, and many are discouraged by one failure after another. Some specialization should be practiced for complete success with this species since it is usually somewhat reluctant to breed regularly in mixed collections. Some birds are too aggressive to suit Gouldians; and others, particularly Zebras and Societies, are overly helpful to a meddlesome degree. As a result, the placid Lady Gould gives up nesting ideas and frequently deserts eggs or youngsters.

The diet should be kept simple. The standard finch fare as described early in the chapter is adequate. Because these birds are somewhat expensive and have a general reputation for delicacy, many people pamper their birds with overly rich diets and carefully regulated temperatures as if they were hothouse flowers. In these cases, the delicacy is artificially induced; problems inevitably do arise. Normal good care and average safeguards encourage robust health in the Lady Gould.

Many Lady Goulds which have been imported from Japan do have some difficulty making adjustments to American aviculture. Some do not survive the acclimation period despite every safeguard. Our water is usually heavily chlorinated, and our foods are different. They are used to greater quantities of greens and smaller cages than the American fancier usually considers average. Some of these problems can be solved simply. Water can be boiled and cooled; extra food supplies can be brought from Japan during the changeover. Smaller cages and greater quantities of nourishing greens can be provided. Even so, many of these Gouldians are very reluctant to accept the small Australian millet which is the basic seed of our finch mix.

When the long adjustment and acclimation period is over, those Japanese imports which have survived often become the hardiest and best breeders of all Gouldians.

Most breeders of Gouldians maintain several good pairs of breeding Society Finches to take over parental duties of rearing any abandoned Gouldian nestlings. Societies are excellent foster parents, but they should not be housed in the same cages or aviaries because they are *too* helpful.

While they are in the nest, baby Gouldians have three phosphorescent turquoise spots at each corner of the beak. Many Australian finches, and even other finches as well, have these spots; but they seem to be more prominent or at least more frequently noticed on Gouldian nestlings. When they emerge from the nest, young Lady Goulds are very dull in color and almost lacking in pattern. Upperparts are drab green, and underparts are dull gray with some pale buff. They do not achieve adult coloring until they are six or eight months of age, sometimes not until they reach a year of age.

As a rule, youngsters should not be moved to different quarters or environments until they reach adult coloring. Many immature birds die for unexplained reasons during this period of greatest sensitivity.

STAR FINCH

The beautiful Star or Ruficauda is one of Australia's most popular finches. At one time it was comparable in price to the Lady Gould, but it is an excellent breeder and is almost as thoroughly domesticated as the Zebra Finch. As a result, the price has gradually dropped. It still is far more costly than the Zebra Finch and not nearly as plentiful.

It is a perfect aristocrat for beginners. It is lovely, hardy, easily raised, and has a very pretty song which it sings quite freely. The size is nearly four inches long including a tail of one and one-fourth inches. Japanese-raised Star Finches experience practically no difficulty in adjusting to our conditions.

The male Star Finch has a bright red covering all the beak, face, cheeks, and throat. The female has less extensive facial areas of red and is therefore easily distinguished. Underparts have olive on the throat and chest, changing to bright yellow on lower chest and most of the abdomen. Prominent white spots are superimposed over the face and chest. These spots are smaller on the facial area and larger on the chest area. Upperparts are olive, except for some dull red-brown on the tail and rose-red on the uppertail coverts.

Easily one of the loveliest of all finches is this exquisitely patterned Shafttail Grassfinch. This species has become rather rare in both the United States and England since Australia's export ban went into effect.

Youngsters lack the red facial area and the prominent spots. Mostly, they are dull olive, darker above and pale below. Red starts to appear on the face in a few weeks and small spots develop shortly thereafter.

SHAFTTAIL

Another of Australia's most handsome beauties is the Shafttail or Long-tailed Grassfinch which is six to seven inches long because of its long tapering tail. The body size is about the same as that of the Lady Gould. The Shafttail is distinctive because of its sharp and smoothly contrasting design rather than its variety of colors.

Outstanding black accents occur on a large circular bib covering the chin and throat, on the lores (that area between the beak and eyes), on the flanks, and on the long tail. The head is soft gray; and body coloring is a soft, pleasant blend of grayish-brown, darker on the upperparts and pale on the underparts.

The male has a larger bib than the female, but this is often difficult to distinguish. To further distinguish sexes, the male sings a small song and dances a comic little jig to court his mate. His beak is also slightly more bold than that of the female.

There are two races of the Shafttail. The only difference between this orange-billed race and Heck's Grassfinch is the bright coral red beak which also gives it the popular name of Coral Billed Shafttail.

Shafttails are also ideal breeders if given uncrowded conditions and standard care as described above. Incubation time is variable because the birds may not start setting right away. Give these birds both open canary nests and enclosed finch boxes.

PARSON FINCH

The Parson is neat and trim and closely resembles the Shafttail in basic pattern. The coloring is only slightly different. The beak is black, and the chest is pale brown instead of soft pale gray. The wings have more of a brown tint, and the overall appearance of the coloring is somewhat flatter and less soft than that of the Shafttail. The body is stocky instead of trim and slim, and the tail lacks the long tapered elegance found in the Shafttail.

There are two races. The Parson Finch has a whitish rump, and the rare Diggle's Finch has a black rump as well as a slightly paler body shading.

Care, feeding, and breeding are the same as for the Shafttail except the Parson basically has more of an insectivorous nature and will require some live food when breeding.

MASKED GRASSFINCH

The very beautiful Masked Grassfinch is a perfect companion for the Shafttail since it has a similar shape with long tapering tail and a quiet, lovely color contrast. The basic coloring is warm and soft pale brown shaded with pastel rose-fawn. Upperparts are somewhat darker than the underparts. The rump is white and ventral area near-white. The tail and flanks are dark brown. Instead of a bib, the Masked Grassfinch has a triangular dark brown facial mask which includes the forehead, surrounds the eyes, and tapers to a blunt end on the throat. The beak is a bright waxy yellow, slightly larger and richer in color on the male. Eyes are deep wine red, and feet and legs are red-orange.

Sexes are difficult to distinguish; but, in addition to the larger beak, the male has a bolder facial mask. He also sings and dances like the Shafttail.

Care, feeding, and breeding are the same as for the Shafttail; but this bird is a very fast flyer and a little more shy. Breeders should not be disturbed during the nesting season.

A rare relative is the White Eared Grassfinch which has pale white ear patches. The beak and general body coloring is also somewhat paler in shading.

OWL or BICHENO FINCH

Popular and active, the sharply patterned Owl is a very distinctive species with a pleasant personality and a size smaller than a Zebra Finch. Though the colors are not greatly diversified, the pattern is outstanding. The white face and underparts contrast sharply with two dark brownish-black bands which contribute to one popular name: Double-bar Finch. One cuts across the lower chest, and the other encircles the face and bands the lower throat area. This encircling feature frames the face and darkens the forehead.

Upperparts are dark brown with tiny white spots arranged in a crisp and sparkling pattern on the wings. The tail and rump are brownish-black. A close relative, the Ringed Finch or White Rumped Owl, has a white rump.

The Owl is difficult to sex, but the male has brighter white underparts and bolder bars. Both sexes should be viewed side by side on a perch to determine the difference.

Owl Finches are very peaceful, and they add great charm to any mixed collection. They are not known as free and easy breeders; but if given a sizable aviary and congenial companions, preferably more Owl Finches, they often become prolific. Care is the same as for Zebra Finches, but they should have some live foods for best results. Most Owls prefer open canary nests instead of boxes and secluded nesting sites, since they are shy breeders.

Youngsters up to about four months are much more neutral in color than their showy parents. Whites are dusky, and the dark areas are pale. The bars are very faint and narrow.

DIAMOND SPARROW

The very handsome Diamond Sparrow, which is not a true sparrow, is the largest of Australia's Grassfinches. It is a stocky bird about five inches in total length with a short square tail. This is a great favorite with bird fanciers because it is peaceful, showy, and an excellent breeder if given proper surroundings and diet.

For best breeding results this rather expensive bird should be given an uncrowded and secluded aviary with a minimum of companions. It is a somewhat shy breeder in mixed company. During breeding periods, overly inquisitive neighbors such as Zebras or Societies may arouse some aggressiveness or may cause desertion of nests. If a nestbox is used, it should be larger than the average finch box.

As with most finches, incubation time is twelve to thirteen days with both parents participating. Youngsters may remain in the nest from eighteen to twenty-two days, but they may not be weaned for another three weeks. The dull and dusty youngsters assume adult coloring very slowly.

The pattern is very attractive. One really bright feature is a brilliant, glossy red area covering the rump and uppertail coverts. The beak is red subdued by a silver-gray cast covering all but a thin rim about the base. Both the base and the tip of the beak are lighter and brighter. The red-brown eye is surrounded by a bare and faintly red ring. The lores are boldly black, and a fine line of black surrounds the eyes.

The head and neck are dull gray shading to pale silvery-white on throat and lower cheeks. Back and wings are dusky grayish-brown, and the tail is black. The underparts are white with sharply contrasting black in a pleasing pattern. A broad black chestband extends down the sides. The sides, partly obscured by folded wings, are crowded with large white spots.

Sexes are very similar, but females have slightly brighter red beaks and larger white spots on the sides.

If Diamond Sparrows are kept in close confinement, they often acquire a feather plucking vice which is difficult to correct.

AUSTRALIAN FIRE FINCH

The vivid and long-tailed Australian Fire Finch, five to five and a half inches in length, is also called the Crimson or Blood Finch. It is not in any way related to African Fire Finches which belong to the Waxbill family. It is expensive, rare, and aggressive. It is not a community bird. Individuals may be peaceful for long periods, but they usually cannot be trusted with smaller species.

Australian Fire Finches are active and beautiful, and well worth the extra space it takes to give each pair a separate aviary. Under such conditions and given a suitable supply of live food, they often become very prolific. Don't give too many mealworms; over-indulgence causes problems which unbalance the rest of the diet. A variety of small insects and a dish of insectile mixture will help fulfill the insectivorous requirements. Mealworms should be rationed to three or four per bird per day and increased when youngsters are in the nest. Incubation periods are variable. Youngsters usually leave the nest when they are about twenty-one days old.

Both sexes are beautiful and glossy, but males are far more outstanding. The male has a brilliant red covering the beak, face, throat, and most of the underparts. On the lower areas of the underparts this red becomes darker and approaches a blackish shade in the central abdominal area, the ventral area, and the undertail coverts. Tiny white spots are scattered on the sides of the chest and flanks.

The upperparts are subordinate in coloring because most areas are mixtures which are darkened by brown except for the rump which is again bright crimson. The long, graduated tail has more red than the back and wings and is therefore brighter.

Females have duller and less extensive red areas except for the large bright red facial patch. The abdomen is dull brownish, and the throat and chest are much duller than corresponding areas in the male.

Youngsters have black beaks and mostly resemble subdued females. Young males show scattered traces of bright red in areas where the adult male is particularly bright.

PLUMHEAD or CHERRY FINCH

The modestly-colored Cherry Finch of four to four and a half inches is also known as the Plumhead Finch. It is not as popular as most of the species mentioned before, but it has been bred in surprising numbers since the Australian ban went into effect. Live foods, rationed mealworms, and a good bland grade of insectivorous mixture are necessary. Oily mockingbird foods cause trouble.

The brightest coloring occurs in a richly vinaceous and glossy dark plum shade which covers the forehead and part of the crown. The male also repeats this color on a small chin bib. Females lack the bib and have smaller crown patches, and the coloring is usually less vivid.

Upperparts are dark earthy-browns slightly tinted with a dull vinaceous tinge. Tail and wings are darker than the back, and a trace of metallic green adorns the shoulders. Some white spots occur on the wings and scapulars, and white and brown mottlings mark the rump.

Underparts are mostly dull white with slender bands of purplish-brown on the sides of chest and flanks. The overall pattern is somewhat cluttered. Immature birds are dull brownish-gray above and whitish-gray below.

Cherry Finches seem to prefer bundles of grasses to nest boxes, and they usually build closer to the ground than do most finches.

FIRE TAILED FINCHES

Both species of the expensive Fire Tailed Finch are very rare and difficult to maintain in captivity. These are really for the advanced fancier, so coverage here will be brief.

The Fire Tailed Finch is pretty but not spectacularly colored. Brown upperparts are suffused with olive green. Both the upperparts and the pale underparts are finely striated with minute dark brown bars. Males show blackish abdominal areas. The beak and rump are bright red, and a blackish facial mask covers the forehead and lores and tapers to a point behind the eyes.

The Red Eared Fire Tailed Finch has a red ear patch below the tapered tip of the mask. The lower chest and abdominal areas are more boldly barred in this species.

SYDNEY WAXBILL

Australia's only waxbill, the Sydney Waxbill, is pretty; but it is dusky and unassuming compared to most Grassfinches. It is not considered to be a good breeder and is therefore bypassed by many bird fanciers.

The Sydney Waxbill is about four to four and a half inches long including the one inch tail. It has bright red on the beak and on the long, broad eyebrows. The rump and uppertail coverts are also red. Some black occurs on the top of the upper mandible. The rest of the bird is mostly dull and soft gray with grayish-green wings, dark tail, and a warm golden-olive across the nape and shoulders.

The male has bolder and longer eyebrows than does the female. Youngsters are dull and dark with no red on the eyebrows and only a trace of red on the rump.

AUSTRALIAN MANNIKINS

The three Australian Mannikins are the lovely Pictorella, the handsome Chestnut Breasted, and the plain Yellow Rumped. The latter is a good breeder, but it is not popular because of its unimaginative color scheme. The others show only fair breeding records. They should be offered a variety of nests and should be in secluded uncrowded aviaries. Some live food and plenty of seeding grasses should be added during the nesting period.

These four and a half inch Mannikins are hardy and peaceful in disposition but bold and robust in appearance because of their thick silvery-horn beaks, short tails, and stocky shapes. The Pictorella and Chestnut Breasted are the most beautiful of all Mannikins, but they are seldom available because of Australia's export ban.

The Pictorella is the most attractive because of its spangled chest. Large white spots overlay a broad black chest. Sexes are easily distinguished because the females have smaller and flatter, almost rectangular spots.

The face and throat are dark brown. The rest of the coloring is subordinate and quiet with subtle changes in shading. This makes a description difficult and elusive. Upperparts are frosty ash-brown with darker shadings on wings and tail. Small white spots occur on the darker areas. Underparts are buffish with irregular and subtle scallops of a darker shade of brown.

The Chestnut Breasted Mannikin has a masculine appearance and is feathered in earthy shades of various browns and buffs. The facial area is dark brown, highlighted with fine golden-yellow streaks radiating outward from the eyes. The crown and nape are frosty, pale brown with fine dark brown streaks. The back and tail are brown, and the rump is bright golden-brown.

The golden-brown chest is separated from buff white underparts by a bold band of dark brown. Some brown bars irregularly mark the flanks.

Sexes are difficult to determine. Males usually have larger beaks and bolder bands across the chest. Fortunately, the males dance often for the females, and this is the most reliable determinant.

The Yellow Rumped Mannikin has as its only bright feature a glossy yellowish-straw on the rump and uppertail coverts. Head, neck, and part of the mantle are pale gray. The back and wings are brown; and the tail is brown with some dull, pale straw color on the two central feathers. Buff underparts fade to near white on the lower underparts.

PARROT FINCHES

All Parrot Finches are Southwest Pacific birds. The Pintailed Nonpariel is the only species imported with any frequency. It is somewhat expensive, but not nearly as costly as the well-known Red Headed or Tri Colored Parrot Finches.

Though all of the better known Parrot Finches are quite beautiful, the writers feel they are somewhat less than ideal. The Pintailed Nonpariel, while lower in price than the others, is difficult to transfer to domestic diets. It is not a good breeder, and the lovely red underparts fade drastically to a yellowish-straw shade unless given a color-holding agent. The others are better breeders and easier to acclimate, and they do not fade in captivity, but they are all tremendously expensive. Moreover, most of them are extremely shy and spend most of their time hidden from view wherever possible.

Pintailed Nonpareils are less expensive at export points where they are considered pests because they raid rice fields. Paddy rice and hulled oats must be soaked in water and fed together during acclimation and slowly transferred onto our standard diets. Before the transfer to canary and white proso is complete, these seeds must for a considerable period be soaked and dried before feeding. Insectile mix and two mealworms per day are advisable. After these acclimation problems have been overcome, the cost is understandably higher but still moderate. It is therefore a popular and worthwhile bird.

The newly imported male Pintailed Nonpareil is lovely. The three inch body length is enhanced by a long tapering tail of two and one-fourth inches. The large beak is black. Upperparts are dark green; the face, throat, and forehead are bright blue. Rump and uppertail coverts are bright red, and the tail is a darker and softer red. Most of the underparts are red, bright on the chest and diluted on the abdomen. Sides are duller, and the ventral area is dull buff.

The reds fade after a while in captivity, but they can be held or restored by adding soya powder or carotene in oil to the diet.

Females and immatures have shorter tails and less vivid colors. Reds are greatly diminished, and greens are darker and quieter. Blue on the facial area is nearly absent.

Red Headed Parrot Finches from New Caledonia are the most attractive members of the family. The head, throat, and part of the upper chest are bright red; the rump and tail are a duller shade of red; the remaining coloring is bright green. The females have slightly less red on top than do males, but this is a difficult distinction. The size is about four and a half inches. Good breeding pairs can be really prolific, but these are very shy birds which desert the nest at nearly any disturbance.

The Red Headed Parrot Finch does not fade in captivity. Its diet is the standard finch mix except for heavier percentages of canary, spray millet, greenfood, fresh fruit, and rationed mealworms.

The Tri Colored Parrot Finch is not as showy as the above species because the blue head is less contrasting and less extensive. Blue does not extend into the chest. The red on the tail is also less vivid. Even so this is an extremely beautiful bird highly coveted by advanced fanciers. Females are slightly less bright than males, especially in the cheek area.

The Tri Colored is even more shy than the Red Headed species, and it is an extremely fast flyer. Care and breeding information are the same as for the Red Headed Parrot Finch.

There are a few other Parrot Finches, but they are seldom available and need not be covered here.

Chapter VI

MANNIKINS

Most mannikins have comparatively heavy bodies and thick beaks compared to other popular finches. As a rule, the average colors are varying earthy browns and blacks with white as the most common color for contrast. The only bright coloring is red, and this occurs only in the Cutthroat and Red Headed Finch. The darker species therefore are excellent contrasts for many of the more colorful finches.

Mannikins are always popular because they are hardy and because they take kindly to captivity. Standard finch fare is ideal, and some of the larger species live and breed very well on the regular budgerigar diet. Cutthroats and Red Headed Finches, in fact, live very well with budgerigars. These are the only species which frequently must be kept separate from many of the smaller species. All the rest are peaceful.

Some mannikins are very good breeders, and some are among the most difficult to entice into the nestbox. Breeding information is the same for all. Practically all, except Society Finches, expect a little live food during nesting operations. Societies sometimes like live food, but most ignore it.

Australian Mannikins have already been covered in Chapter V.

SOCIETY or BENGALESE FINCH

Perhaps the most interesting member of this chapter is the prolific Society Finch which in Europe is called the Bengalese. This is a very inexpensive domestic species which in its present form does not occur in the wild state. It came about as the result of a series of hybrid breedings in China centuries ago. No one any longer knows its true parentage although, by comparison, several species were obviously used in its evolution.

Societies are four and a half inches long including a broad tapered tail of one and one half inches. No two are identical in their mottled patterns. The basic colors are chocolate-brown, cinnamon, and white. Chocolate and white mixtures predominate with cinnamon and white also prevalent. Occasionally a blend of chocolate and cinnamon mixed with white occurs. Some individuals are all white, all chocolate, or all cinnamon. The latter two are called *selfs*. Pure whites are recessive to both shades of brown and are somewhat weaker and less prolific than the others. Moreover, some whites show a tendency to blindness if they are not frequently outcrossed to birds with some brown in their plumage.

Many Societies are crested. To obtain good crests, mate a crested bird to a crest-bred bird. A crest-bred bird is one which does not have a crest itself, but one of its parents was crested. Mating crested to crested brings about baldness in Societies.

Societies are difficult to sex by observation. In most mannikins, the males have larger beaks than do females. Physical characteristics in Societies are not pronounced; the only accurate way of determining sex is to wait for the courting display. In this comic performance the male stretches his head up in the air, puffs out his chest, and sings a squeaky little song to the female. The song is punctuated by short vigorous hops. Fortunately, the display is frequent. Since nesting periods may occur at any time of the year, the nuptial display is not restricted to any season.

Either covered wicker nests or nestboxes are satisfactory for Societies. They nest as well in cages as they do in aviaries. They are ideal foster parents for many of the rarer finches which are more difficult to breed. Most finch fanciers who specialize in rare finches maintain several pairs of Societies in separate cages to take over as foster parents if the real parents fail in their domestic duties. The incubation period is thirteen days, and hatching time of adopted eggs should coincide as closely as possible to the hatching of their own eggs.

In mixed aviaries Societies and Zebras are overly helpful in community nesting operations. They frequently move in with any bird who happens to be nesting. This is not at all an aggressive act, but most other birds do not appreciate such meddling. As a result they may abandon all interest in raising a family.

SPICE FINCH

Though there are several subspecies with slight variations, the only steadily available race of Spice Finches comes from India. The smaller and darker Philippine Spice Finch has been imported frequently the past few years. Both races are very inexpensive and very hardy. They are ideal for beginners, and, though they do breed in captivity more easily than most mannikins, they cannot be called prolific. Nestboxes are preferred, and incubation time is twelve to thirteen days.

Spice Finches from India are slightly over four inches long including the one-inch tail. Sexes are similar, but the black beak is larger in the male than in the female. The head and all upperparts are a rich warm brown. Underparts starting with the upper chest area show a fine lacy network of brown scallops overlying the dull white background. The center of the abdomen and ventral areas are dull white.

Youngsters are a dull, smoky brown. Mature plumage is assumed in blotches.

The smaller Philippine Spice is perhaps less attractive because there is less contrast, and the brown is not as warm and glowing. The underparts have far less white. Instead of a bright spangled appearance, the dusky white scallops look more like short, irregular streaks. The beak is mostly pearl-gray with considerable black on the upper mandible. This race is extremely difficult to sex by the beak. The most accurate method of determining sex is to watch for the display dance which is similar to that of the Society.

A few Indian Spice Finches may become aggressive with small waxbills. These individuals are better kept with larger weavers and Java Rice Birds. Most, however, are very peaceful.

NUNS

Three species of nuns are regularly available to bird fanciers. All have the same modest requirements and are very hardy. Standard finch fare is adequate, and live food is optional. Most pay no attention to it. All are peaceful, but very few show any inclination to breed in captivity. Toenails on these birds grow long in captivity and need frequent clipping to safeguard against entanglement in wire netting. The size is about four inches including a one inch tail. The thick silvery-gray beak is bolder and more massive in the male. Youngsters are

More popular in England than the United States, Magpie Mannikins are to be found in isolated African shipments.

uniform grayish-brown, and mature colors come in blotches in much the same manner as in Spice Finches.

The inexpensive Black Hooded Nun from India is somberly colored in dark, glossy brown and black. A black hood covers the entire head, neck, and upper chest area. Brown covers all the rest of the bird except for a blackish concentration extending from the center of the abdomen to the ventral area. Bright red-brown, heavily glossed, highlights the rump. The Philippine Black Hooded Nun is slightly smaller and has a slight brownish tinge along with the black.

The Tri Colored Nun from India has one simple change to brighten it considerably. The chest and flanks are bright white. The price is usually only slightly higher than the price of the Black Hooded Nun.

The White Headed Nun is not often available and is somewhat higher in price. It is like the Black Hooded Nun except the head and neck are white. This species is more easily sexed because the female's white has a dull, somewhat dusty appearance.

SILVERBILLS

There are two species of Silverbills, neither of which can be described as attractive. Both, however, are popular because they are plentiful, inexpensive, hardy, and because they are excellent breeders. The diet is standard and no live food is needed. Both are about four and a half inches long, including the sharply pointed tails. The silvery-gray beaks of both species are larger in males. Males also perform the typical little song and dance nuptial display which is characteristic of most mannikins. Nesting information as well as diet are the same as for the Society or Spice.

The Indian Silverbill is more attractive than the African species because of greater contrasts. Upperparts are brown with very dark tail and flight feathers. White covers the rump and uppertail coverts. Underparts are whitish with a shade of buff on the chest.

African Silverbills are more of a uniform buffish brown all over with only a slightly darker shade on the wings and tail. The rump too is brownish. Both species hybridize freely, and cross-bred offspring have pinkish rumps.

BRONZE WINGED MANNIKIN

The small and lively Bronze Winged Mannikin from Africa is frequently available at a very reasonable price. Its small three and one-fourth inch size, which includes a one inch tail, coupled with a sharp pattern and friendly manner, help to make it distinctive and popular.

The Bronze Wing is rather a good breeder in mixed collections. Standard finch fare plus a little live food and plenty of greens comprise the simple requirements. Incubation lasts for twelve to thirteen days, and youngsters fledge in about three weeks. Youngsters are mostly dull brown above and grayish below.

Bronze Wings are neat and trim without the heavy appearance and thick beaks of most mannikins. The upper mandible is black and the lower mandible is pearl-gray. Upperparts, including head, neck, and upper chest are all dark brown. Wings and tail are darkest. The head is bronzed with a concentrated metallic cast on the crown. A deep metallic green patch highlights the shoulders. The rump, sides, flanks, and undertail coverts are attractively and irregularly scalloped with brown on white in a lively manner to relieve the generally somber appearance. The remaining underparts following the chest bib are bright white.

Sexing is difficult. The size of the beak is often too similar to be distinct. The bronze gloss on the crown, usually stronger in the male, must be viewed in just the right light to tell the difference. Behavior is the truest test. Males sing and hop for the females.

CUTTHROAT

Easily one of the most beautiful and readily available of all mannikins is the popular Cutthroat or Ribbon Finch, which is a robust bird approximately four and a half inches long. It is a good breeder and is hardy, but it occasionally is aggressive toward smaller birds. Wherever this tendency manifests itself, which is more frequently during the nesting season, the overbearing individual should be transferred to aviaries containing larger finches. The Cutthroat has also been housed successfully with Budgerigars in many instances.

Cutthroats always catch the eyes of beginners because of the broad gash of brilliant red across the throat of the males. Cutthroats especially enjoy performing their nuptial display. The dance is more vigorous and more frequent than is customary with most mannikins. Cutthroats are good breeders. Breeders are usually more successful if the nestbox is slightly larger than average size. Some live food is also advisable during the breeding season.

The thick mannikin beak is pale horn in color. The plumage is an earthy mosaic of pinkish-browns with buff, gray, and blackish accents irregularly camouflaging the whole scheme. Underparts are paler than most of the upperparts, but the chest has a considerable amount of the warm pinkish-brown. The female is slightly less bold in general markings and lacks the bold red gash under the throat. Youngsters are like females, but they lack the pinkish-brown shading in their plumage.

RED HEADED FINCH

The rather large Red Headed Finch from South Africa is the aristocrat of the family. It is seldom available and rather high in price, but it is attractive and extremely hardy. There is a noticeable relationship between the Cutthroat and the Red Headed Finch. The general basic coloration is very similar, but the chest is more distinctly spangled with white spots. The male has a deep rust-red covering the head, chin, and nape. The female is similar except the head has the general body color instead of red.

The Red Headed Finch is about five inches long including a tail of one and three-fourths inches. The blunt beak is broad at the base; the head is quite large for this stocky, heavy-bodied bird.

Chapter VII

WAXBILLS

Most waxbills are small, nervous, alert, and active. They have small, sharp beaks and pleasing personalities. Nearly all are extremely peaceful, and most are reasonably hardy after an initially delicate acclimation period. Some become feather pluckers if crowded, but this can be corrected by separating those individuals from their own kind and housing them in a large aviary. Very few can be considered good breeders; but many are among the most popular, charming, and inexpensive of all imported finches.

It should be emphasized that many waxbills are very delicate for at least two weeks after importation. It is therefore important that your birds be properly acclimated before you purchase them.

During the nesting period live food is necessary if success in rearing youngsters is to be attained. At other times live food is advisable but not necessary with all species except those specifically mentioned. Insectile mixture is a helpful supplement to the diet at all times but is most important while youngsters are in the nest. Incubation is twelve to thirteen days, and youngsters leave the nest when between seventeen and twenty-one days old. Variable weaning periods extend from one to two weeks.

One waxbill comes from Australia and has already been mentioned. Strawberry Finches come from India and the Orient. All other waxbills are native to Africa, but not all will be covered in this book because some are too seldom available. The St. Helena Waxbill has been introduced into many islands in the South Pacific and into South America where it is thriving. Some importations from South America contain "Brazilian Waxbills," but these are actually St. Helena Waxbills. The waxbills most frequently available at the lowest prices come from Senegal. East African and Angolan species are slightly higher, and those from South Africa are nearly always expensive.

INDIAN STRAWBERRY

Both the Indian and the Chinese Strawberry go through a seasonal color change, and these are the only waxbills which do. During the six month eclipse phase, many of those coming from India are tinted various colors.

Some of these are called Painted Finches, Green Strawberries, Painted Strawberries, and perhaps by various other fanciful names. It is therefore perhaps wise for the bird fancier to be able to recognize the various finches whose names may be appropriated for these tinted Strawberries. For instance, many bird fanciers have bought green-tinted Strawberries thinking they were the true Green Strawberry only to be disappointed when the tint faded out. The true Green Strawberry is considerably more expensive and not often available.

The Indian Strawberry is a great favorite with bird fanciers because it is inexpensive and hardy and is nearly always available. Moreover, it has a lovely little song.

Newly imported Avadavats such as these are quickly acclimated with reasonable good care. The male (on the left) while in color has red on the chest and head, and bold white spots sprinkled generously on chest and wings. The female has straw-colored underparts and dull brown upperparts.

The size is slightly more than three and a half inches long including the one inch tail. Males in color have rusty-red covering the head, chest, abdomen, and rump, with small white spots sprinkled generously on the wings and chest. Upperparts are dull brown. Both sexes have red beaks.

Females and males out-of-color have a dull and dark yellowish-straw shade replacing the red areas. The white spots disappear from the chest but remain on the brown upperparts. The red stays on the rump to make sex differentiation possible. The male always retains a brighter red in this area than does the female.

The Black Throated Wattle Eye (*Platysteira peltata*) from Africa is one of those great rarities which is seldom available even to zoos. The female on the left has the black covering nearly all the throat and chest whereas the male has a rather narrow black band across the chest. All other underparts on the male are white. Wattle Eyes are Flycatchers which are extremely difficult to maintain in captivity without great quantities of live foods in as wide a variety as possible. Its care is similar to that required by the Paradise Flycatcher.

The four and a half inch Blue Tit or Titmouse *(Parus caeruleus)* of Europe is a vivacious and acrobatic personality which is rarely kept in captivity. In many European countries it is protected by laws and can neither be kept in captivity nor exported. The Blue Tit is one of the most attractive of all the Tits, with its lovely rich shades of blue and frosty bluish-white around the facial areas. The Blue Tit is delicate during acclimation stages until it learns to accept domestic diets. As with Japanese Tumblers, the diet is omnivorous. Sexes are alike, but the female is less vivid in coloring than the male.

Youngsters are often imported too. They are soft and dull brown, paler on the chest and without white spots.

CHINESE or ORIENTAL STRAWBERRY

The slightly more expensive and not as often available Chinese or Oriental Strawberry is a little smaller in size, but it has a much richer shade of red. Everything else is the same.

GREEN STRAWBERRY

Also known as the Green Avadavat, the Green Strawberry from India is seldom available and somewhat costly by comparison. The size is about four inches including a one inch tail. The beak is very deep but very bright red. Upperparts are a bright shade of dark green, and the tail is blackish. Underparts are yellow, brightest on chest and abdomen. Sides and flanks are boldly marked with alternating black and white bars in a prominent accent. Face, cheeks, and throat are a dull shade of greenish-yellow.

Sexes are similar except the female is duller in greens and yellows, and the black and white bars show less contrast.

Green Strawberries are prone to feather plucking. Since this is a difficult habit to overcome, it is wiser to have no more than one pair per aviary.

This species is not considered a good breeder. Live foods, in a variety if possible, are beneficial at all times.

AFRICAN FIRE FINCHES

The lovely and inexpensive Senegal or Common Fire Finch is imported every year in large numbers. It is an ideal waxbill for novice or experienced fanciers and is always popular. Comparatively speaking, the Fire Finch is the best breeder of the waxbill family. Live food and nestling food are necessary for this success, but otherwise the standard finch fare is adequate.

Fire Finches should go through a strict acclimation period before they are sold or else they cannot be considered hardy.

Sexes are very different in coloring. Size is three and three-fourths inches long including the tail which is nearly an inch and a half long. Both sexes have red beaks. The male is deep glossy red on the head and chest fading to dull brown at the lower end of the abdomen. Several small white spots occur on the sides of the chest. The upperparts are dark brown except for the bright red rump and traces of red near the shoulders. A fine yellow eye ring is prominent in fully mature males.

Females are all brown, darker above and paler below, except for the red rump and red on the lores and over the eyes. White spots on underparts are slightly more numerous than on the male. Youngsters are like the female, but they have no red and no white spots.

Several races of Fire Finches show very minor variations. Both Jameson's Fire Finch and the Blue Billed Fire Finch have darker rose-red shades and dark beaks. Females instead of being brown are more like the males in a much duller shade. There are other species of Fire Finches, but they are rarely available and are not suitable for novices. These are detailed more extensively in *Finches and Softbilled Birds*.

CORDON BLEU

The equally popular and perhaps even more beautiful Cordon Bleu is an ideal companion for the African Fire Finch to show the contrasting beauty of both species. The lovely shade of sky blue and a slightly longer tail to add an aura of gracefulness are very distinctive features. Cordon Bleus are nevertheless inexpensive.

The male has lustrous sky blue on face, cheeks, and much of the underparts. From the center of the lower chest the remaining underparts are dark tan. Except for the blue tail and uppertail coverts, the uppersides including forehead and crown are mouse-brown. The male also has a vivid maroon ear patch. Both sexes have beaks of soft rose with gray tips.

Females and immatures have no cheek patch and there is less blue on the chest. Youngsters have darker beaks than adults.

Newly imported Cordon Bleus are delicate and must go through an acclimation period similar to Fire Finches before they are hardy. Breeding success is not as frequent as with the Fire Finch, but the procedures are the same.

Blue Capped Cordon Bleus from South Africa are starting to become available from time to time, but they are expensive. This rare species is perhaps a little hardier and easier to breed. The male has blue covering the entire head and nape which gives this species the illusion of having a larger head. The beak is a brighter shade of rose with no gray tips. The female has some blue on the forehead. This feature plus the all rose beak marks the only distinctions from the female Blue Waxbill.

The Blue Waxbill or Angolan Cordon Bleu is like the common Senegal species except it has no maroon cheek patch, and the brighter but lighter blue is a little more extensive on the underparts. Beaks are very slightly darker in both species. The female is otherwise like the other Cordon Bleus. Blue Waxbills are slightly more expensive than the red cheeked variety, but they are hardier and easier to breed.

RED EARED WAXBILL

The least expensive waxbill is the lively, tail twitching Red Eared Waxbill. It is always popular and usually abundant. It is three and one-fourth inches long including the one and one-fourth inch tail.

The basic pale brown coloring is overlaid with a very attractive rose cast. Uppersides are darker brown, and underparts are pale with the rose shading very prominent, especially in its heaviest concentration on the abdomen. The bold tapering eyebrows and the beak are bright red. The rump and tail are black.

Sexes are very similar, but the male has a broader eyebrow and more rose on the abdomen. Red Eared Waxbills are not usually interested in breeding in captivity.

This very hardy species requires the standard finch fare.

A similar species is the Crimson Rumped Waxbill which is not often imported. It is less attractive because the rose glow is absent, and the overall appearance is dull and flat by comparison. The black beak has a hint of red on the lower mandible, and there is an added red on the wing coverts and rump.

ST. HELENA WAXBILL

Several very similar races of St. Helena Waxbills occur over a large area of Africa, but none are imported as regularly or as inexpensively as the Red Eared Waxbill. The St. Helena is like a somewhat more flamboyant Red Eared Waxbill. The Greater St. Helena Waxbill is about one and one-fourth of an inch larger than the Red Ear, and the entire body is covered with prominent but finely drawn darker brown striations which are most noticeable on the chest.

A heavy concentration of rose starts on the center of the chest and extends to the central abdominal area where it changes to black which continues through the underside of the tail.

The Bicheno or Owl Finch from Australia has in the past few years become exceptionally rare in aviculture in the Western Hemisphere. The failure of aviculturists to establish this species firmly as a domesticated and free breeding bird before or just after the Australian export ban went into effect is deplorable. Formerly quite moderate in cost, it is now one of the more expensive of the Australian finches. Though a number of fanciers are breeding this species, those few who have been successful have been unable to supply the demand for this lively and beautifully patterned charmer. Photo by Horst Mueller.

The Pearl Headed Amadine (Odontospiza caniceps) from Eastern Africa is also known as the Pearl Headed Silverbill. It has only recently become available to bird fanciers. It is more closely related to Silverbills which it resembles in most characteristics except for the far more attractive pattern and coloring. Sexes are alike, but the male is slightly richer in coloring and has larger white spots. The courting dance of the male is, as in the Society Finch, a more reliable indication of sex.

The beautiful Gold Fronted Chloropsis is an extraordinary songbird in spacious, well planted aviaries; but the brilliant green often blends with the leaves of the plants. However it is easily tamed and becomes completely confiding even in aviaries.

Males have bolder striations and broader eyebrows than females, and the rose on the lower chest is richer. Youngsters lack the striated pattern and are devoid of rose or red.

Many bird fanciers are successful in breeding St. Helenas. Procedures and requirements are the same as for Fire Finches and Cordon Bleus.

ORANGE CHEEKED WAXBILLS

The pretty Orange Cheeked Waxbill has a vivid red beak and a large, bright orange cheek patch covering most of the facial area. Upperparts are mostly dull but pale brown. The rump is red and the tail is grayish-black. The head is dark gray fading to pearl-gray on throat, chest, and most of the underparts. An overlying concentration of orange occurs on the central abdominal area.

The female has a paler beak, a smaller cheek patch, and less orange on the abdomen. However, since these colors fade slightly after awhile in captivity, these differences, except for the beak, may not be completely reliable.

General care is the same as for all the above birds. This species cannot be considered as being a good breeder.

GOLD BREASTED or ORANGE BREASTED WAXBILL

The very popular Gold Breasted Waxbill is the smallest and one of the most beautiful of all waxbills. It is just three inches long including a one inch tail. Sexes are different, but both male and female have red beaks, brown upperparts, orange rumps, and blackish tails.

The male has bold orange-red eyebrows and golden yellow underparts with bright orange undertail coverts. The chest varies among individuals and is comparatively dull until adulthood, at which time it flares up like a vivid sunset with bright orange and red-orange. The sides are faintly barred with brown and yellow.

Females lack the orange eyebrows and colorful chests. They are nearly identical to female Strawberry Finches except for the smaller size, orange rump, and some orange on the undertail coverts. Youngsters are like females.

The Gold Breasted Waxbill is a fair breeder, but success is variable. Environment and companions exert a great influence on whether or not the breeding season will be productive. Live foods are important too. Care and required diet are typical of the rest of the waxbills.

The South African Gold Breasted Waxbill is a larger, rarer, and more expensive subspecies. It is not as attractive because the coloring on the chest is greatly reduced to a very pale orange. The zebra markings on the sides are bolder.

LAVENDER WAXBILL

Another popular and very attractive waxbill is the three and a half inch Lavender Finch which has a one and one-fourth inch tail. Soft and smooth pearl gray covers all except rump and tail which are deep red. A few white spots are scattered on the flanks and sides. This simple color scheme never fails to attract admirers, and it is a favorite with most finch fanciers despite its poor showing as a breeder and despite the fact that some individuals are affected by melanism while others become addicted to feather plucking. The melanism and feather plucking can usually be corrected with proper care.

Lavenders are very difficult to sex, but males usually show slightly more red on the back and in the ventral area. In the nuptial display the male holds a fluffy feather in his beak and waves it up and down in front of the female. This is the most reliable indicator.

BLACK CHEEKED WAXBILL

Among the rarer and quite expensive waxbills is the dignified and graceful Black Cheeked Waxbill which comes from South Africa. This long-tailed beauty has a very precise and smoky color scheme. The four and a half inch length includes two inches of tail.

Upperparts are smoky-mauve with distinct and crisply drawn narrow bars of alternate dark and light shades on the wings. The tail is black above and grayish-black on the underside. The darkly subdued deep red on the rump reaches around to brighten the sides and abdomen. The chest is paler than the upperparts and shows an almost hidden trace of dull rose-mauve. A large smoky-black facial patch dominates the head. The nearly black beak has a pearl-gray base.

Sexes are difficult to distinguish, but the male has bolder striations on the wings. The Black Cheeked Waxbill is not a good breeder, but it is well worth a try. An isolated pair in a planted aviary would have the best chance of success, especially if a variety of small live foods were available.

BLACK CAPPED WAXBILL

Also from South Africa and also rare, the Black Capped Waxbill has a lively personality and an unusual pattern. It is slightly less than four inches including a tail of approximately one and one half inches. The black beak has red at the base of the lower mandible and in fine lines on both sides of the upper mandible. A sharp, black cap covers the top of the head. Underparts, face, throat, nape, back, shoulders and scapulars are gray with a pale shade on the undersides and a duskier smoky shade above. The flights and tail are black. The striated or barred effect of the Black Cheeked Waxbill occurs on the shoulders and scapulars. A vivid flash of bright red covers the rump and uppertail coverts.

Sexes are extremely difficult to tell apart. The striations are slightly bolder on the male, but behavior is the only true test. Youngsters have dull brown on the back and wings, dusty buff on the underparts, and no striations. The writers have found no reports of breeding success in captivity, but chances would be better if these birds were given accommodations as described for the above species.

DUFRESNE'S WAXBILL

Another rare beauty from South Africa is the ever active Dufresne's or Swee Waxbill which has the same tail twitching mannerisms of the Red Eared Wax-bill. Though slightly heavy-bodied, Dufresne's is still shapely in its three and a half inch size including a tail of one and one-fourth inches.

This species is slightly prone to feather plucking if they are crowded. Though not considered reliable breeders, youngsters have been reared several times. Live foods, especially a variety of small insects, are necessary and seclusion in a planted aviary is advisable. Other information and statistics are the same as for waxbills. Youngsters resemble females but have less green on the wings.

Uniformity of shading and sharpness of contrasts are responsible for Dufresne's great beauty rather than flashy colors.

The red rump is the only sizable bright accent, but the lower mandible of the beak is also bright red. The upper mandible as well as the feet and legs are black.

Head and nape are smoky-gray shading softly into black which covers most of the face and cheeks as well as the throat on the male. The lower boundary of this black area is sharply divided from the pale pearl gray which extends through the chest before it changes to an indistinct but soft straw color on the

Zebra Finches are among the most productive of all breeding birds in captivity. The male is very attractive with the bright cheek patch, chestnut flanks with white spots, and zebra lines on the chest. The female lacks these features and usually does not even have the indistinct dark markings on the chest shown in this picture. Photo by Harry V. Lacey.

The beautiful Blue Tit of Europe *(Parus caeruleus)* in a less alert pose. This is the puffed pose usually assumed during rainstorms when it shelters itself in crevices or huddles in fissures in tree trunks.

rest of the underparts. The folded wings hide olive on the sides. The back and wings on the uppersides are also olive. The red rump contrasts sharply with the black tail.

Sexes are easily determined because the female lacks the black on the face and throat.

Several subspecies, all called Yellow Bellied Waxbills, have more of a distinct yellow on the abdominal area; but both sexes lack the black facial area. These then are similar to female Dufresne's Waxbills, but the male has more yellow.

VIOLET EARED WAXBILL

The undisputed king of the waxbills is the rare Violet Eared Waxbill whose extraordinary beauty cannot effectively be described. This expensive, graceful, and long-tailed rarity from South Africa is a close rival to the Lady Gould even though it is less flamboyant. It glows with a richness and warmth that cannot be captured even by the color camera.

The size is a little over five inches long. The male is resplendent in rich, deep reddish-brown on head, back, and wings which varies from chestnut on the head to darker near-brown on the primary flights. The uppertail coverts are brilliant dark blue, and the grayish-black tail is edged in dark blue. Chest and underparts are bright burgundy-brown fading on the abdomen and ventral areas.

The head is especially variable. The beak is bright wine red, and the reddish eye is surrounded by a bright red ring. The forehead is vivid blue, and a long chin and throat accent is black. A large cheek area covering most of the face is purplish-blue in an unbelievable richness.

The female has dull, pale brownish upperparts except for the bright blue uppertail coverts. Underparts are bright fawn from the throat downward with a tinge of red spread on the chest and upper abdomen. The head is subdued in intensity, but the shadings are still attractive. The cheek patch is paler, and the blue on the forehead is barely present.

Breeding success is very rare. The standard finch diet plus live foods, insectile mixture, seeding grasses, and greenfood are all important. Mealworms should be rationed, and other live foods should consist of a variety of small insects. They must be taught by other birds to accept the insectile mixture. Other requirements and statistics are typical of all waxbills. Because these are expensive and rare, the owners usually are not careless or neglectful with these birds; but they should also be careful not to pamper them into weak hothouse flowers.

PURPLE GRENADIER

The closely related Purple Grenadier from South Africa is also expensive and rare. It has a heavier body which tends to lessen its shapeliness.

The head of the male is similar to the Violet Eared Waxbill, but the cheek patch is greatly reduced, and the blue forehead and black throat are absent. Back and wings are more brown, and the rump is cobalt blue. Vivid purplish-blue covers all of the underparts from the chest through the undertail coverts. Some uneven chestnut markings on the underparts detract from the overall uniformity.

The female is brownish, paler on the underparts and shaded with chestnut on the head. A bold whitish patch surrounds the eye, and white spots are sprinkled generously on the underparts. The blue rump contrasts with the blackish-gray tail.

PYTILIAS

The members of the genus *Pytilia* are a departure from most waxbills in that they are larger and have heavier bodies and longer, narrower beaks. They are highly insectivorous, and should be given a variety of small insects as well as rationed mealworms. Three mealworms per day is sufficient, but this can be at least doubled during nesting. *Pytilias* take to insectile mixtures quite easily. Except for the Aurora, few *Pytilias* have been successfully reared in captivity. Other care and vital information is standard as for most waxbills.

MELBA FINCH

The delightful and rather expensive Melba Finch or Green Winged Pytilia is the most highly coveted and most beautiful member of the genus. The male is an excellent songster, rivalling some of the musical softbills in quality if not in volume.

The five inch size includes a tail slightly less than two inches long. The male has bright coral-red on the beak, head, and throat. Soft gray divides this area in the vicinity of eyes and lores. Lower crown and neck are gray changing into dark olive-green on back, wings, and rump. Uppertail coverts and the upperside of the tail are dull red with blackish on the underside.

A rich golden-olive wash occurs on the throat and upper chest followed by olive overlying the basic gray which covers the rest of the underparts. Irregularly shaped white spots and fine black lines are tightly packed on the lower chest becoming larger on sides and flanks.

The female has soft gray replacing all the red on the head and the golden-olive on the lower throat and upper chest. Her white spots begin at the lower boundaries of the throat.

Melbas are calm and reasonably hardy after the touchy acclimation period. Few problems arise if correct diet and properly rationed mealworms are supplied. Some individuals become feather pluckers, and an occasional male might be temperamental and aggressive especially if confined to small cages with others. There are a few minor variations in the several subspecies.

RED FACED WAXBILL or ORANGE WINGED PYTILIA

The Red Faced Waxbill is dark and somber compared to the Melba, but it is still highly coveted because it is rare. It is like the Melba in shape but is nearly an inch smaller. Most of the body coloring is a deep, dull olive with a brighter shading of burnt-orange on the outer webs of the flight feathers which, when the wings are folded, is very prominent. There is also a tinge of burnt-orange on the chest. The center of the abdomen is white in an irregular pattern; there are some wavy white lines or irregular striations on the chest, flanks, and undertail coverts. The tail and uppertail coverts are like the Melba's tail.

Perhaps the brightest feature is the red on the head of the male covering beak, forehead, crown, face, and chin. The female has gray in these areas.

Habits and diet requirements are the same as for the Melba.

AURORA WAXBILL or CRIMSON WINGED PYTILIA

The simply patterned and quietly colored Aurora is the same size as the Melba. Dietary requirements are similar, but it is a better breeder. Most of the coloring is soft gray which is finely barred on underparts and neck with alternating shades of lighter and darker grays. The beak is slate-gray. Bright crimson covers the rump and upper side of the tail as well as a broad band starting with shoulders and covering most of the primary flights.

Females can be rather easily distinguished because of the less distinct striations.

In the past few years Red Headed Finches from South Africa have frequently become available. Females lack the red on the head and the well-defined spots on the chest. This species is larger and more dominant than its relative, the Cutthroat or Ribbon Finch. It should not, in most instances, be kept with smaller finches. Photo by Horst Mueller.

African Glossy Starlings, of which there are several species, are richly iridescent and are very attractive. Moreover, they are extremely hardy and easily maintained on a standard softbilled diet. Mynah pellets are an excellent single unit food for them if the bird fancier wishes to simplify diet to the ultimate. These Green or Blue Eared Glossy Starlings, now called *Lamprotornis chalybaeus*, may, because of their heavy iridescence, show color variations due to angle of lighting; and the several similar species and subspecies can easily cause confusion in avicultural identification. Photo by Horst Mueller.

The Red Faced Aurora or Yellow Winged Pytilia has golden-yellow instead of red on the outer webs of the flights, and the male has a red facial area similar to that of the Red Faced Waxbill. This is an exceptionally rare species.

TWIN-SPOTS

Twin-Spots are like Pytilias in general requirements and in shape including the long slender beak which denotes an equally insectivorous nature. All are rare and expensive, and all have large white spots boldly scattered across chest and flanks. Breeding success is more frequent with Twin-Spots, but each breeding is still a noteworthy achievement.

Peter's Twin-Spot is the most beautiful. The chest background is black. On the male, extensive and rich crimson covers all facial areas, sides of the neck, and throat down to the chest. A fine-lined eye ring of greenish-blue is a bright contrast. The beak is slate-gray; and the forehead, crown, and nape are grayish-brown shading to brown tinged with red on the back and wings. Rump and uppertail coverts are deep red, and the tail has both red and black in it.

The female has less red on the face and throat.

The male Green-Backed Twin-Spot has bright red on the face and dark olive green on the rest of the head, throat, and uppersides. The wings are dusky, and the rump is tinged with yellow. The tail is olive-green in the center and black in the outer areas. The ventral area is pale olive-buff, but the black chest and white spots are similar to those of Peter's Twin-Spots. Females have dull orange instead of red in the face. Two subspecies show slight variations.

The Brown Twin-Spot has a rich chestnut on the underparts instead of black, but the white spots are still just as bold and somewhat more numerous. Males have small crimson throat patches and females have white throat patches. The gray of the head changes to brown on the back and wings. Rump and uppertail coverts are dark red, and the tail is black.

Dybowski's or Dusky Twin-Spot has an extensive area of deep crimson starting on the broad mantle and covering back, rump, and uppertail coverts. The male has a black background with white spots on underparts, and the female has more of a gray background. The rest of the coloring is subdued in slaty or dusky shades.

Chapter VIII

WHYDAHS AND WEAVERS

Both weavers and whydahs are flamboyant families which are rather closely allied. Except as otherwise noted all males go through a plumage eclipse during which they resemble the drab sparrowlike females in dull buff and straw with dark streaks. During the six to eight months of their in-color phase, the colors and patterns of the weavers are brilliant. Those weavers which have red in their coloring fade to bright orange after a season in captivity due, presumably, to the lack of certain live foods in the diet. This does not affect health in any way.

Whydahs, except for the Combassou, grow long tail feathers which are particularly distinctive in the finch family. The length of these tail feathers becomes progressively longer until maximum length is reached during the fourth year. Most whydahs during their first season in color do not grow long tail feathers. The basic coloring is black with some attractive and variable accents. Whydahs are often called "widow birds" in Africa because of their long flowing tail feathers. All are presumed to be polygamous in the wild state.

The diet for all of these birds is the standard finch fare with live foods and plenty of greens. Many of the larger species may be given parakeet mix instead of finch mix. After acclimation, all are very hardy and long lived. All of these birds are from Africa with the Baya Weaver as the one exception, and none breed well in captivity.

In the wild state many weavers build huge "apartment-house" nests with great colonies flocking together. Their talent for weaving grasses into nests is quite astonishing. Many whydahs are "parasitic," which means they lay their eggs in other birds' nests. Several of those which are not parasitic have been reared in captivity on a few occasions. Whydahs have interesting and ebullient courting displays which make full use of their long fluttering tail feathers in gaining attention from the females as they fly high into the air and back.

Most weavers and whydahs are rather large and usually aggressive. As a rule, they should never be mixed with small waxbills or Australian finches. The Paradise Whydah is an important exception and is ideal in a group of small birds.

Not all weavers are important to aviculturists. Many are bypassed because they are not colorful or because they are too aggressive. Some are just never available, and some require enormous amounts of particular live foods which cannot be supplied in captivity.

Sexing birds in this chapter is very difficult if the males are out of color. Minute inspection for traces of nuptial coloring is sometimes effective if the period of inspection is either closely before or shortly following the in-color seasons. At other times, it is mostly guesswork. Males in color are usually far more costly than males out-of-color, but they are worth the extra price. In

The Ruddy Ground Dove (*Columbigallina talpacoti*) ranges from Mexico to Argentina and is about six and a half inches long. The female has less brown and more gray on the upperparts and is also more gray on the underparts. This is one of a group of several small doves which can mix with finches in an aviary. Photo by Horst Mueller.

Many different species of the group of Mannikins successfully hybridize with Society Finches, and the appearance of the offspring usually cannot be predicted. Even nestmates often vary considerably. These hybrids are nearly identical to Philippine Spice Finches except for the richer shade of brown. The writers, however, do not know the actual parentage.

whydah importations most birds are shipped out-of-color, but even so males usually far outnumber females.

PARADISE WHYDAH

A male Paradise Whydah in full nuptial costume is an unforgettable sight with its two broad black central tail feathers which eventually reach fourteen inches in length. Two large black paddle shaped feathers of two and three-fourths inches in length are added distinctions. The actual body length is three and a half inches, exclusive of tail.

Black covers the back, wings, tail, beak, head, and throat. A glossy chestnut collar extends onto the chest and fades into pale buff which covers the remaining underparts.

Females and males out-of-color are mostly sparrowlike in dull buff. Two wide blackish bands run lengthwise down the top of the crown and several indistinct darker markings occur on the upperparts. Males have slightly bolder bands on the head and are slightly larger.

Some species of whydahs are very similar when they are out-of-color, but the Paradise Whydah seems to have a larger and flatter head perched upon a longer neck than most members.

This species in the wild state lays its eggs in the nest of Melba Finches.

The rare Buff Naped Paradise Whydahs from South Africa have pale buff in a broader and more disctinctive collar.

Broad Tailed Paradise Whydahs have shorter tail feathers, but they are much broader. The body is heavier, and the chestnut shade is more glossy and much greater, extending down onto the lower chest.

Both these latter forms are equally as peaceful as the regular Paradise Whydah, but they are seldom available and are a little more costly.

Taking everything into consideration, the Paradise Whydah is one of the most ideal of all finches. Despite its exotic appearance, it is very reasonable in price. Novices and advanced fanciers alike consider it among their great favorites.

PINTAILED WHYDAH

The second most popular whydah is the inexpensive and regularly available Pintail Whydah from Western Africa. Though it is considerably smaller than the Paradise, it should not be mixed with small finches because it is very aggressive during the breeding season.

Both sexes have red beaks at all times except while they are young. Females and males out-of-color otherwise resemble female Paradise Whydahs except they are smaller and do not have such long necks and flat heads. Males have almost imperceptably bolder head stripes.

The male in color is beautiful. Four long black central tail feathers, which ultimately reach nine inches, are slender and ribbonlike. A large black cap and a small black chin patch accentuate the red beak which is brighter while he is in color. Black from the shoulders extends in a broad bar down to the sides of the chest. Most of the flight feathers are black except for a white band across primaries and scapulars. Except for the tail, the rest of the bird is white.

QUEEN or SHAFTTAIL WHYDAH

A close relative to the Pintailed is the rare and extremely unusual Queen Whydah from South Africa. The male in color is the same basic pattern as the Pintailed except underparts are buff instead of white, and the four long tail feathers are bare shafts with prominent spatulated feathery tips. The beak is red.

This male Pintail Whydah is nearing its full color phase. Some traces of brown still occur in the black areas of the head and wings, and the tail has not yet reached its full length. The changeover from its drab out-of-color plumage occurs remarkably fast.

The body is slightly smaller than that of the Pintailed Whydah. Males out-of-color and females are more buffish than the Pintailed, and the dark head stripes are nearly absent. Though more peaceful than the Pintailed Whydah, it is nevertheless more aggressive than the Paradise Whydah.

FISCHER'S WHYDAH

Fischer's Whydah from Eastern Africa has been unavailable for many years, but it is now sometimes mentioned on exporters' lists. It also is a relative of the Pintailed and Queen Whydahs.

The Greater India Hill Mynah is one of several very similar subspecies which are very talented talkers. In recent years, nearly as many of the subspecies *intermedia* have been exported from Thailand as from India. Youngsters are usually hand reared in their countries of origin, and when they reach the marketable export age they are delightfully tame birds. The subspecies from Thailand, if anything, now receives better hand rearing than the same race in India and is equally adept at learning to talk. This is an adult male with long wattle flaps and highly lustrous iridescence. Photo by Horst Mueller.

Green Cardinals are excellent aviary birds and are the best breeders of the Cardinals. The female, not pictured, is much duller in color than the male especially in the dominant black and yellow shadings. Photo by Horst Mueller.

The long, slender central tail feathers of the male in color are yellowish-straw. The head cap is yellowish; the rest of the head, throat, mantle, back, and chest are glossy black. Remaining underparts are dull yellowish. The rump and uppertail coverts are buffish with blackish streaks, and the beak is red. Remaining upperparts are similar to those of the Pintailed Whydah.

Males out-of-color and females are like female Queen Whydahs with less black in the markings. Dispositions are also similar to those of Queen Whydahs.

RESPLENDENT WHYDAH

Also rare and from Eastern Africa, the Resplendent Whydah is sometimes called the Longtailed Combassou. The male in color is almost completely glossy black like the Combassou, but it has four long slender black central tail feathers. A few white touches occur on the sides of the rump, on the tip of the tail, and on the undersides of the wings. Iridescent purples, blues, and greens highlight the glossy black.

Females and males out-of-color resemble Pintail Whydahs, but the beak is brownish-horn instead of red.

COMBASSOUS

The jet Combassous, also called Steel or Indigo Finches, are classed with whydahs despite the lack of long tail feathers. They are parasitic in nesting habits like many whydahs, and they go through eclipse plumage. When out of color, the males resemble females, and both look like miniature female Paradise Whydahs. The size is three and three-fourths inches including a tail of one and one-fourth inches.

Males in color are shiny black with purple and blue iridescence. The beak becomes a paler horn shade. This makes a wonderful color contrast to a White Zebra. Combassous are usually reasonable in price and are regularly available, but they are not among the most popular finches.

A few individuals become aggressive during the breeding season; it is wise for the bird fancier to remain alert if he houses Combassous in mixed collections of small waxbills. Most, fortunately, remain peaceful.

JACKSON'S WHYDAH

The heavy bodied Jackson's Whydah from Kenya is about five to six inches in length. When in color, the male has many very luxurious and long tail feathers which he obviously seems to enjoy because he displays often in his strutting and flamboyant manner. The elongated neck feathers are raised in a weaver-like ruff during this erotic display. Surprisingly, this species is non-parasitic.

The male in color is nearly all black except for the brownish wings which have pale scalloped edges. Much of the black is highlighted by glossy iridescence.

Females and males out-of-color are typically sparrowlike in their drabness, but the male is slightly larger and more brownish.

Jackson's Whydahs are very rare and quite expensive, but fanciers always feel they are worth the search and the price.

GIANT WHYDAH

Equally distinctive, the Giant Whydah from South Africa is also rare and expensive and, despite its larger size, is peaceful with even the smallest finches. The male in color is one of the most lavishly ornamented of all whydahs. The body is approximately seven inches long, and the eight to twelve long, broad, and supple tail feathers are graduated in length with the two central ones reaching up to an ultimate of eighteen inches. The longer than average flight feathers are needed for the curiously graceful and undulating flight. Except for the wings, all the coloring is black, sometimes velvety and in some areas glossy.

Wing feathers have brownish margins, and a red shoulder patch fades to red-orange in captivity.

Out of color appearance is typically drab and sparrowlike, but the wings are a little darker than average, and some of the wing patch coloring is retained. Males are a little larger than females.

Giant Whydahs are non-parasitic and are seldom reared in captivity. Even so, the male displays frequently.

RED COLLARED WHYDAH

The occasionally available and handsome Red Collared Whydah has a body length of three and a half inches exclusive of tail. All of the long tail feathers, usually twelve in number, are three-eighths of an inch wide and are approximately the same length. Those which the writers have owned have had tail feathers six and a half inches long. Older birds in all probability may attain a length of eight inches.

Most of the male in color is black including the beak. Pale brown margins occur on secondary flight and covert feathers, and a red-orange half collar extends across the throat.

The Red Collared and its handsome relatives listed below, all of which are non-parasitic, should be housed with weavers and larger finches. Few, if any, of its close counterparts are readily available, but they are well worth the trouble it takes to get them. The Long Tailed Black Whydah lacks the red collar. The Red Naped Whydah has a wider collar and red on the head.

There are several other whydahs of this same genus which have shorter and comparatively stiff tails. All are non-parasitic and few are available with any frequency. The body sizes are about the same as that of the Red Collared, and they should also be housed with larger finches. These birds all have some coloring either on the wings or on the back. The Red Shouldered Whydah has red or orange-brown epaulettes, and the Marsh Whydah has yellow shoulder patches. The Yellow Backed Whydah has a broad yellow area on the back. White Winged Whydahs have some yellow as well as white on the wings, but the white is usually mostly hidden. Yellow Shouldered Whydahs are similar, but they lack the white.

ORANGE WEAVER

The popular, inexpensive, and colorful Orange Weaver is the most frequently available of all weavers. Even though not quite four inches long including its one inch tail, this species is a little too aggressive for small finches.

Males in the wild state are brilliant red and black, but the red in captivity fades to vivid orange which remains as one of aviculture's most brightly colored birds.

The head is velvet-black to the back of the crown. A brilliant sweep of orange covers the nape of the neck, the lower facial area, throat, and chest. The longer nape feathers are tinged with red and are slightly recurved to give a fleecy erectile ruff. Back and scapulars are deep and less bright orange-red. Flights and coverts are brown with pale margins. The rump, upper, and lower tail coverts are elongated, lacy, and filmy covering most of the brownish tail. Lower chest and abdomen are black.

The female and the male out-of-color are streakishly brown above and warm buff below. The warm earthy coloring has a high degree of smooth uniformity compared to Napoleons and most other weavers.

The male Orange Weaver which is imported in its native color of brilliant red is frequently called the Grenadier Weaver. This is a mistaken assumption

Cutthroat or Ribbon Finches are among the most ideal of finches for beginners in aviculture, and they usually retain their popularity among the advanced students of aviculture. The female lacks the ribbon of red and has less boldness in other color patterns. Photo by Harry V. Lacey.

The Pagoda Mynah (*Sturnus pagodarum*) from India and Ceylon is an attractive and very hardy aviary bird. The black cap is actually a recumbent crest not always raised. This species and all members of the genus *Sturnus* cannot be imported into the United States, but many species are popular in Europe because of their bold personalities, maintenance ease, and low cost. They should not be mixed with small softbills. The diet is the simple fare accorded to all mynahs. Photo by Horst Mueller.

by those who do not realize the difference from the native red and captive orange. The Grenadier Weaver also fades in captivity. Since it comes from South Africa where shipments are infrequent, it is seldom available. It is similar but slightly larger. The orange extends to the top of the crown, and the black of the face covers the chin and throat.

The larger and heavier-bodied Crimson Crowned Weaver is four and a half inches long including a tail of one and one-fourth inches. In this very similar species, the orange also starts at the top of the crown, and the black facial area also extends to the chin and throat. The orange stops at the beginning of the chest giving far more extensive black on the underparts. This species is even more aggressive than the Orange Weaver.

NAPOLEON WEAVER

The perfect counterpart for the Orange Weaver is the black and yellow Napoleon Weaver. The price, availability, popularity, size, and disposition are nearly equal.

The male in color has a wing pattern similar to that of the Orange Weaver, but the edges are paler. The tail is also brownish. Black covers the beak and a large facial area including the chin and throat. Yellow flares across the chest and covers the sides and undertail coverts. The large central area of the chest through abdomen and ventral area is velvety black. Yellow also covers the upperpart of the head, the lower back, rump, and uppertail coverts. The neck ruff is partially erectile.

When out-of-color the male has the typical weaver-like pattern, but the basic yellowish-straw color is more cluttered with dark streaks on the back and chest than the Orange Weaver. There is a distinctly yellowish eyebrow. Sexes cannot be distinguished during out-of-color phase.

There are several similar but not as attractive races of the Napoleon Weaver. Very few are ever imported. The Taha Weaver and a few other races have no yellow on the underparts.

MASKED WEAVERS

There are numerous varieties of Masked Weavers which frequently become available. Most have basic similarities in that they are mostly yellow and have black on the face. The sizes vary considerably as does the amount of black in the face. All have typical brown wings with pale buff margins on most of the feathers. Females and males out-of-color are all similar.

The Little Masked Weaver is the smallest and one of the prettiest. The size is not quite four inches long including a tail of slightly more than an inch. The black facial area is more extensive than in most Masked Weavers covering forehead and part of the crown as well as the throat. There is a greenish shade on the back, and the yellow has a sharp lemon cast.

The Half Masked or Vitelline Weaver is the most typical and most frequently available of a large group of very similar Masked Weavers. It is a robust four and a half inches including a one and one-half inch tail. The black facial mask is broad across the cheeks, but it covers only a very small chin area and a very narrow forehead band. A shade of reddish chestnut enhances the crown and base of the throat. The wings are decidedly more brownish.

The attractive and large Rufous Necked Weaver has an intimidating size of more than six inches with a short tail. Bold and fearless, it is much too aggressive even for most large finches. It is best housed with budgies and medium-sized, hardy softbills. It should not be put in a planted aviary because it will defoliate every plant in its tireless and continual passion for weaving.

In truth, this is a remarkably admirable bird because of its uncommon strength and hardiness. One cannot help but admire its many unique and interesting characteristics, but there are few collections in which this bird will safely fit except with Budgies. It lives happily on a standard parakeet diet plus mealworms or other live foods. It also is quite fond of sunflower seeds.

The male in color is similar to the Half Masked Weaver described above, but the entire head and a deep V-shaped throat termination are dark brown which almost appears to be black. The nape fades to reddish-brown or rufous. The black beak is long, and the dominating eyes blaze with red. The back is rather dark, and the wing feathers are edged in yellow.

The Rufous Necked Weaver does not revert to the typical weaver-like drabness when it goes out of color. The brightness is, however, greatly reduced; the head fades to an olive-yellow shade while the beak turns to a pale horn shade. During the breeding season the female nearly undergoes a plumage change. The head assumes a slight shade of olive, and the underparts become more yellowish.

RED BILLED WEAVER

The bold, aggressive, and extremely hardy Red Billed Weaver has a very different and attractive coloring during the breeding season. The male in color has a becoming and vivid shade of rose on the top of the head, neck, and most of the underparts where it fades in the vicinity of the lower chest and abdomen. A large black facial area includes an extensive throat area and a thin forehead band. The wings, back, and tail are typically weaver-like with brown feathers and pale margins. The feet, legs, and an eye ring are reddish; and the large beak is a deep shade of red.

When it goes out-of-color the beak retains a pale reddish shade. The female is also rather distinct in that the large beak is brighter in pale yellowish-buff.

The Red Billed Weaver is frequently available and is usually rather inexpensive, but it cannot be housed with small birds. It is excellent with larger finches and even Budgies.

BAYA WEAVER

The Baya Weaver from India is the only weaver from outside Africa with which bird fanciers might become familiar. It is occasionally imported in large numbers, usually either by error or by substitution but sometimes because its cheap price intrigues inexperienced importers. It usually is an all around disappointment. It has recently even been available in tinted colors in several variety stores.

SCALY CROWNED WEAVER

The small and charming Scaly Crowned Weaver from South Africa represents a complete departure from all the weavers described in this book. It does not undergo a plumage eclipse, and it rarely is aggressive. The writers have always kept it with waxbills and have experienced no problems. The four inch size includes a tail of one and one-fourth inches. Usually this species is a little expensive, and it frequently is delicate at first. However, after acclimation, it becomes quite hardy.

The basic coloring is gray, darker above and paler below, with unique black and white contrasts. The beak is pale pink on the upper mandible and whitish-pink on the lower mandible. The lores are black, and the eye-rings are white. A broad black walrus mustache gives a comically dour expression. All the feathers on the top of the head are black with finely-etched white margins giving a fine-lined scaled effect. The wings and tail have the same pattern.

There are several species and subspecies of African Orange Weavers. The male on the left is the standard avicultural subject which bird fanciers call Orange Weavers and which ornithologists more frequently call Red Bishops (*Euplectes orix* or sometimes *Pyromelana orix*). Perhaps one of the most attractive of the Red Bishops is the Crimson Crowned Weaver (*Euplectes hordacea*) in the upper right side of this picture. This species and its subspecies are widely distributed in Africa but are not frequently available to bird fanciers. Females of all three species are very drably colored. Males when not in color as shown here resemble females during the non-breeding season.

The Black Crowned Waxbill from Central Africa is a very handsome species, but its two most attractive features do not appear in this photograph. The rump and uppertail coverts are brilliant red. The scapulars and shoulders are finely barred with alternating paler and darker shades of gray and dusky black.

The Southern White Breasted Rail (*Laterallus leucopyrrhus*) occurs in Brazilian and more southerly areas in South America. It is a charming, attractive, and very peaceful addition to aviaries containing finches or small softbills. Omnivorous in diet, small rails such as this species require insectile mixtures as well as mealworms. The writers also feed some raw meat. Rails, often called Crakes, belong to a large family of birds which vary greatly in size, characteristics, and food requirements. Related genera and species are native to most areas of the world.

Chapter IX

BUNTINGS

Buntings in American aviculture are quite rare. Most of the best ones are not to be found on the market because they are native to the United States and are therefore illegal. A few filter into the hands of American bird fanciers, and many are shipped to Europe where they are highly coveted and admired. Those buntings native to Europe and Asia are less than ideal because they are not colorful and because their aggressiveness makes them difficult to place safely in the average collection.

New World Buntings should be given a far greater percentage of plain canary seed than is found in the standard finch or parakeet diet. Parakeet mix may be used in place of finch mix because these birds are larger than most of the small finches. Spray millet, fresh fruits, and live foods are also important in the diet. Mealworms are avidly accepted, but should be rationed. Buntings should be taught to take insectile mixture along with the above diet.

None of the birds in this chapter are good breeders. Incubation time is about thirteen days, and fledging time is twelve to thirteen days. This period is short because of the large quantities of live foods consumed by these birds while nesting.

Old World Buntings are, despite their lack of popularity, extraordinarily hardy. They easily adapt to nearly any diet and thrive under conditions which would destroy most birds.

RAINBOW BUNTING

The most important bunting in aviculture for Americans is the lovely five inch Rainbow Bunting which is native to Mexico. The male is a beautiful bird, but the female is dull by comparison.

There is considerable misunderstanding in sexing the Rainbow. Females are very rarely imported, probably because Mexican exporters feel they are too colorless to be saleable. As a result, most people see only the males in quantity and assume the sexes must be identical.

The male seldom fails to attract attention with his lovely glossy blue upperparts and his bright, cheerful yellow underparts. The chest has a concentration of orange overlying the yellow, and a cap covering forehead and crown is bright green. The large, dark eye is surrounded by a pale yellowish eye-ring.

The uninspired color scheme of the female has a dusky shading of yellowish-green on the underparts and grayish-green tinged with blue on the upperparts.

Because of the dietary changes listed above, the bird fancier should bypass this species unless he is willing to devote the slight extra attention required to maintain its long life and good health. Not given this extra care, the Rainbow usually will not have a long lifespan.

PAINTED or NONPAREIL BUNTING

In Europe, the Painted Bunting is a great favorite and is rather expensive. It is a native of Mexico and the United States and therefore cannot legally be kept in captivity here. The five and a half-inch Painted Bunting is hardy and quarrelsome with other buntings. It is difficult to breed.

Males have a richly diversified and bright color scheme. Brilliant purplish-blue covers the head down to the shoulder. The dark eye has a fleshy-orange ring around it. The mantle and back have a bright chartreuse saddle, and the wings and tail are dark green with some dull purplish-red in the scapulars. Rump and lower back are bright red. Underparts starting with the chin are bright red fading in the ventral area. After a time in captivity, the reds fade to dull pink.

The dull female has a grayish-green shade which is darker on the uppersides and paler, more yellowish on the undersides.

INDIGO BUNTING

The deep and dusky blue Indigo Bunting, also a native of the United States, undergoes an eclipse plumage during which the coloring fades to a dull brownish shade above and a buffish shade below. In eclipse plumage, the male resembles the female except some blue shadings remain, particularly in the wings. When he is in color, he has a pleasant glossy sheen with a shade of violet in the head.

Indigo Buntings are about five inches long and are hardy. They take to aviary life very well, but they are not good breeders. In European aviculture, these birds are great favorites.

LAZULI BUNTING

Also a native of the United States, the Lazuli Bunting is much like the Indigo Bunting except it is slightly larger and has a different coloring on the underparts starting with the chest. The chest is brownish-orange fading to whitish on the abdomen and undertail coverts. There are also two whitish bars on the wings.

During its eclipse plumage, the male resembles the female, which, in turn, closely resembles the Indigo Bunting. The Lazuli is also a poor breeder in captivity.

YELLOW BUNTING or RED HEADED BUNTING

The Yellow Bunting from India is one of the misfits mentioned earlier in this chapter. It is a long and slender seven inches in length. This is a shapely bird because of its long tail, but it still is not very attractive. The head of the male, despite the popular name of Red Headed Bunting, is rich brown fading to buffish-brown on the nape and mantle. Back and wings are brown with pale margins on many of the feathers. The rump and tail are brown shaded with gray and black. Underparts are variable shades of dull yellow.

The female is grayish-brown with traces of green and dark streaks on the back. Females are seldom imported.

The Cordon Bleu, an African Waxbill, is one of the most popular and attractive of all the birds which fanciers call finches. The female lacks the maroon patch on the side of the head and has less extensive blue in a quieter shade.

The Redpoll (*Carduelis flammea*) is a native of Europe as well as North America and cannot be kept in captivity by American fanciers. It resembles European Linnets in many respects. The red marking on the forehead and crown and the black chin are distinguishing features. There are slight seasonal differences in color, mainly the addition of a pinkish shade on the chest of the males which fades in captivity. Sexes are similar, but the female has diminished areas of red on the head and lacks the pinkish shades on the rump and chest. The general care and feeding are the same as for European Linnets, siskins, and serins. Redpolls are often hybridized with other closely related birds. Despite their drabness, Redpolls are good aviary birds because of their activity and amusing antics. Their song is not spectacular. There are several species of Redpolls which differ very slightly in coloring and size. This species is about five inches long. Photo by Dr. Jesse.

Chapter X

EUROPEAN FINCHES

This chapter includes some of the popular finches which are imported from Europe every fall. It does not cover all of them. All the birds in this chapter are comparatively inexpensive except the European Bullfinch which cannot legally be imported. It does, however, become available from time to time and is popular with advanced fanciers.

EUROPEAN BULLFINCH

The male European Bullfinch has an exceptionally beautiful color scheme and a sharp, well contrasted pattern. Plumage has a smooth uniformity not found on other European birds. The most eye-catching feature is a beautiful shade of smooth rose-pink covering underparts from the throat to the abdominal area where it fades to dusty grayish-white on the rest of the underparts. Jet black covers the rather large beak, the lores, a small chin, and a large black cap which extends to the nape and abruptly changes to soft gray which covers most of the upperparts. The wings and tail are black except for a grayish-white bar on the scapulars. Feet and legs are also blackish.

The female has the same pattern, but the rose-pink on the underparts is changed to a lovely soft shade of gray.

The size is a little less than six inches. The shape is a little strange and bullet-shaped because of the broad and flat head and no indentation for the short neck.

Bullfinches require a different diet if they are to remain healthy. In addition to a mixture of parakeet seeds and canary mix, it needs fruit, buds, and a variety of insects instead of just mealworms.

Some Bullfinches are aggressive to smaller birds, but they are not active enough to be safely included with other large finches who might also be aggressive.

CHAFFINCH

Quietly colored and mild-mannered, the highly active Chaffinch is frequently overlooked by American aviculturists because of its unassuming appearance. It is peaceful to all birds despite its comparatively large size of five and a half inches which includes a tail of two and one-fourth inches. The Chaffinch is a robust singer during the spring in the wild state, but it does not sing frequently in a cage or aviary. The song has perhaps more volume than melody, but its cheerfulness is unsurpassed.

Chaffinches are hardy and thrive on parrakeet mix, finch mix, or canary mix which shows it is adaptable to most conditions. It also likes greenfood but pays little attention to live foods. Chaffinches are often used in hybrid breedings with canaries or other European finches.

The soft and subdued color scheme of the male is difficult to describe because of the many soft traces of additional shadings. Face, throat, and underparts are a

Both sexes of the European Bullfinch share the same feather pattern, but the body color of the male (left) is rose, whereas that of the female is gray.

dull blend of rose, gray, and brown fading to dull off-white on abdomen and undertail coverts. The top of the head and nape are a pale shade of gray with some hints of blue-gray. The dark grayish wings are accented by sporadic white markings. Traces of moss-green crop up on the neck, wings, tail, and very prominently on a large rump area.

The female, which is very rarely imported, is subdued in almost every way. The basic pattern is there, but most hints of rose and moss-greens are absent. The underparts are a dull, flat, pale brown.

EUROPEAN LINNET

The pleasant song of the European Linnet is just about its only important feature. It is peaceful and is coveted for hybrid breedings with canaries, but it is not hardy in the United States and has a plain appearance. During the acclimation period, it is delicate and falls prey to many disorders.

The male is dull brown, darker and streakier on the upperparts and paler and smoother on the underparts. Blackish wing feathers show some white borders on the primaries. Some deep reddish-maroon traces occur on the forehead and chests of wild birds, but these fade out in captivity.

The female is slightly paler with fewer white accents on the flights and more streaks on the chest.

The writers feed canary mix, niger, oat groats, greenfood, and a little insectile mixture. Oats, used heavily after arrival, are tapered to small amounts if the birds are to be kept in cages.

EUROPEAN GREENFINCH

The large and heavy-bodied European Greenfinch totals six inches in length. It is aggressive during the breeding season and should not be housed with small birds. After importation these birds are rather delicate, but they adjust well and will thrive on canary mix, some parrakeet mix, a little oat groats, a few sunflower seeds, and plenty of greenfood.

In the group of Buntings, the Rainbow Bunting is the most popular member for American aviculturists. There are more beautiful species in the group, but they are either quite rare or are denied to American aviculturists because of their native status. Males, such as the one pictured, greatly outnumber females in importations. This is unfortunate because fanciers usually want pairs. Exporters apparently send more males because they feel the females are so uninteresting in color that they will not find a waiting market. Photo by Harry V. Lacey.

The rare Red Crested Touraco from Angola (*Tauraco erythrolophus*) is a very attractive member of an unusual family. This individual has damaged plumage, but most Touracos usually have excellent plumage and are very well groomed. Moreover, their long tails add grace to a well-shaped body. Touracos are extremely active birds, and the brilliant red in the flight feathers of most species can be seen to best advantage while the bird is flying. Photo by Horst Mueller.

Chapter XI

GOLDFINCHES, SISKINS, AND SERINS

All the birds in this chapter are noted for song which, of course, varies with the different species and, to some extent, even with individuals. There are several rarely available species which are not included in this book which are nevertheless interesting to many people. Most are given more extensive treatment in *Finches and Softbilled Birds*.

Interest in many of these birds circulates mainly around the hybridizing potentials. Many of these birds are cross-bred with canaries or other members of this group to produce male singers which often sing better than either side of the family. This is a highly specialized branch of aviculture. If canaries are to be used, the female is usually the canary; the male is the outcrossed species. Incubation time is thirteen days, and cup-shaped canary nests are preferred. Most will breed better in planted aviaries, but hybrid breedings are usually more successful in cages. Aviary breeding for mules is successful only if there are no other birds present. Hybrid matings are formed as last resorts as far as the birds are concerned. They prefer their own species for breeding but will accept another species if they feel their own kind will not be available.

There are two main diet divisions to this chapter. The diet for the first group is detailed under the European Goldfinch, the second, under the Green Singing Finch.

EUROPEAN or BRITISH GOLDFINCH

The favorite of all European birds is the European Goldfinch, a truly delightful bird. It is pretty, hardy, a fine songster, and a reasonably good breeder.

Males are more often imported because many are used to cross with canaries to produce mule singers. These mules, while not attractive, are usually magnificent singers. Female mules are worthless because they do not sing and, like most mules, are infertile.

European Goldfinches are about five inches long and are shaped like a canary except that the black-tipped beak is longer and sharper. A fine blackish line surrounds the beak and includes the lores. A large facial area of bright red includes the top of the crown and encircles downward to include the chin and part of the throat. This is followed by white on the rest of the face and is bordered by a blackish band. Nape, back, mantle, and chest are dusky-brownish fading to whitish on the abdomen. Tail coverts, both upper and lower, are white. Wings and tail are black with some white tips. The second bright feature is an irregular broad band of bright yellow on the wings.

Sexes are similar, but the adult male has black on the forepart of the wing between the shoulders and the bend of the wing. The female shows soft grayish-brown in this area. Youngsters also show this shading for quite a long time; but, if they have already attained the red faces, the feathers will show black tips in the maturation process. Some people feel that males can be distinguished by greater amounts of red in the face, but this is unreliable since there is some fading in captivity.

The diet has two phases: one for the acclimation and adjustment period, and another which is slowly adjusted by the following spring for the breeding season. The first phase consists almost exclusively of niger and oat groats. The writers also include gleanings of sunflower seed when cups are emptied from parrot cages. This fulfills the need for hemp seed which in some states is illegal.

As spring approaches, canary mix is accepted, and the quantity of oat groats is reduced. Of course, other requirements such as grit, greens, and canary song food are always given right from the beginning. During the breeding season, nestling food is also important.

Siberian Goldfinches are not as often available and are higher in price. They are identical except for a noticeably larger size.

EUROPEAN SISKIN

Though not as attractive or as good a singer as the European Goldfinch, the four inch European Siskin is always popular and usually becomes calm. Diet and other care is the same as for the Goldfinch, but oat groats should be fed sparingly after acclimation because this bird easily becomes overweight. Females are very seldom available. In appearance they are duller and have no black cap.

The male is mostly a dusky grayish-green, heavily and haphazardly streaked with blackish especially on upperparts. Black accents are prominent in the wings and on an irregularly-shaped patch atop the head.

EUROPEAN SERIN

The European Serin is more closely related to the Green Singing Finch than to siskins, but it requires the same diet as the European Siskin and even closely resembles it. It lacks the black cap and is darker. Both sexes have dark streaky marks on the underparts, but the male has a concentration of yellow on the central chest area.

BLACK HEADED SISKIN

The South American counterpart of the European Siskin is the Black Headed Siskin which is very slightly larger. For the most part the pattern and coloring are very similar, but it is more distinctive because the head and throat down to the chest are all black and the underparts are more yellowish.

COLOMBIAN BLACK SISKIN

Certainly one of the most beautiful of all siskins is the Colombian Black Siskin which is precisely patterned and sharply divided in its bright colors. The well-proportioned size is four and a half inches including its tail which is a little longer than the shorter tails of most siskins.

The male has jet black upperparts from the forehead through the tips of the tail, and underparts are uniformly bright yellow starting with the chin and fading slightly on the ventral area. A pale eye ring is the only accent.

The female has dull greenish-gray replacing the black, and the yellow is greatly reduced.

There are several subspecies with less pleasing variations in the pattern.

VENEZUELAN BLACK HOODED RED SISKIN

The vivid and beautiful Venezuelan Black Hooded Red Siskin is now very rare and is about the most expensive of all finches. It was formerly imported in great numbers to hybridize with the canary and was instrumental in producing the Red Factor Canary, but a Venezuelan export ban now prohibits trapping.

Gouldian Finches are considered by most people to be the most beautiful of all finches. The male in this photo is hiding most of his brilliant chest. Since the Australian export ban went into effect, avicultural sources for Gouldians have mostly been through bird fanciers who specialize in this species or from Japanese imports. Recently some of the problems regarding Japanese imports have been solved; and by special and prolonged acclimation periods, which mostly involve food processing and gradual changes in diet, several importers are having great success with Japanese bred Gouldians. Prior to this advance, most of the imports from Japan would not change to foods available in other countries. It is interesting to note that there are more Red Headed Gouldians than Black Headed Gouldians now available in this country. Photo by Harry V. Lacey.

The male African Fire Finch is a favorite member of the Waxbill family and is inexpensive. It ranks alongside the Cordon Bleu in popularity, but it usually is a better breeder. There are several subspecies and closely related Fire Finches.

The four inch male is richly garbed in brilliant, deep red and vivid black. Black covers the head, nape, throat, shoulders, flights, and tail. The rest of the bird is red, slightly shaded with blackish on the back and fading to white on the abdomen.

The female is mostly gray with some red shadings on the chest, flanks, scapulars, and uppertail coverts, and some black on the tail, flights, and a bar across the upperwing area.

GREEN SINGING FINCH

Africa's best known serin is the popular and cheerful Green Singing Finch which is four inches long including a tail of one and a half inches. It is usually associated in aviaries with waxbills and thrives on the standard finch diet with none of the variations listed for the European Goldfinch except a little extra canary song food. All the following birds in this chapter follow the same dietary pattern. Nestling food should be given during the breeding season. Incubation lasts for twelve to thirteen days, and youngsters fledge in about three weeks.

The male is bright yellow on the underparts and greenish-gray on the upperparts which lack uniformity and smoothness. A prominent yellow eyebrow band connects across the forehead. Gray covers the lores and flares out behind the eyes. The bright yellow lower cheek area is separated from the chin by a dark, narrow mandarin mustache which flares outwards and downwards from the lower mandible. The rump is also yellow.

The female is duller and less distinct in all colors and patterns. Moreover, she has a necklace of ill-defined dark spots encircling the lower throat area. Youngsters resemble females but have underparts of rather dull greenish-yellow. At an early age, young males show a breakthrough which eliminates some of the necklace spots.

A slightly larger cousin from South Africa is called by such names as Yellow Eyed or Yellow Crowned Canary and St. Helena Seedeater. It is somewhat more robust in appearance because of its larger body, larger head, broader eyebrows, and bolder markings. It is an exceptionally vigorous singer with a voice of high quality.

Shelley's Seedeater, also called the Uganda Brimstone Canary, is also from Africa. It is five inches long including its tail of two inches. It has the same basic Green Singing Finch pattern; but the markings are less precise, attractive, and colorful. The yellow cheek patches and the mandarin mustache are absent.

This species and its similar races, Sharpe's Seedeater or Kenya Brimstone Canary, and the Brimstone Canary or Sulphury Seedeater, are expensive, rarely available, and not as hardy as the Green Singing Finch.

GRAY SINGING FINCH

The beautiful, frequent song of the Gray Singing Finch from Africa adequately compensates for its dreary, cluttered gray coloring. Though smaller than the Green Singing Finch, it has an aggressive personality and must be housed with weavers, Java Rice Birds, and other bold birds. Sexes are similar. To distinguish the male, the bird fancier must wait for the song. Fortunately, he sings often. Breeding and dietary information are the same as for the Green Singing Finch.

Close relatives and similar races are the Yellow Rumped Gray Singing Finch with its trace of yellowish on the rump, and the Black Throated Canary which also adds a blackish marking on the chin along with blacker markings on the wings and tail.

Chapter XII

MISCELLANEOUS FINCHES

This chapter gathers the most important members of the other finch families which are popular in aviculture. The standard finch diet is appropriate for all these birds, but parrakeet mix is also acceptable for some. Live foods and insectile mixture are necessary for a few, but these will be mentioned wherever needed.

JAVA RICE BIRD

Easily one of the most popular and best known of all finches is the beautiful Gray Java Rice Bird. Many bird fanciers started this fascinating hobby with a pair of these hardy, low priced birds which are often called Java Temple Birds.

The sharply patterned Gray Java Rice Bird is a heavy-bodied bird of five and a half inches including a tail which is just over an inch in length. They are sometimes aggressive with small birds and should be housed with weavers, Saffrons, Cutthroats, and certain whydahs. They even fit in well with Budgerigars and Cockatiels and will accept a parrakeet diet even more readily than they accept finch mix. Live foods are not required even while nesting.

Sexes are alike, but the huge beak is even larger and bolder in the male. The beak is deep rose-pink fading to whitish at the tips. Feet, legs, and a fleshy eye ring are also pinkish; the eye-ring of the male is a deeper shade of reddish-pink. Males have a pleasant little song and an amusing little courting dance punctuated with frequent hops and a strange whirring sound uttered while waving their beaks from side to side and up and down. Three or four males sometimes indulge in whirring and swaying concerts for their own amusement.

The head is black except for a large, sharply defined, very white cheek patch covering most of the facial area below the eye. The body is gray with a uniform soft slate shade on the upperparts and chest fading to a paler shade on abdomen and gradually reaching a whitish shade in the ventral area and undertail coverts. The tail is black. The uncluttered uniformity and pleasantly balanced contrasts are heightened by a lovely sheen.

Youngsters are dull gray with paler underparts and just a hint of rose in their beaks. During this immature stage, youngsters can be finger trained in much the same manner as Budgies. For a complete and detailed account of this procedure as well as breeding information see our little booklet titled *Java Temple Birds*.

White Java Rice Birds are all white with a glowing, glossy sheen except for the bright pink and red of the beak, eye ring, feet, and legs. In some individuals an occasional dark feather indicates a nearly suppressed pied factor, but most people still call these individuals White Javas which, by the way, are not albinos. Youngsters usually show extensive areas of buffish-grays which change to white as the birds mature.

Calico or Pied Java Rice Birds have variations in which many areas of the basic pattern of the gray variety are replaced by white blotches or mottling.

Many hybrids are not very attractive; but this specimen, which resulted by a mating of a European Goldfinch to a European Bullfinch, is a beautiful bird. It is also a difficult achievement. Photo by Horst Mueller.

The Pied factor in Zebra Finches, as in nearly all birds which have the pied mutation, is very irregular in pattern and often not as attactive as these pictured, particularly when the amount of natural coloring greatly exceeds the white areas. Photo by Horst Mueller.

The male Scarlet Chested Sunbird (*Chalcomitra senegalensis*) from Africa has brilliant red as its main color feature with iridescent green in a subordinate degree on the head and chin. The female is dusky olive-brown with bronzy highlights on the upperparts and paler shades of yellowish-brown on underparts. Photo by Harry V. Lacey.

They appear to be hybrids between the gray and white varieties, but this is not the case. Pied Java Rice Birds and White Java Rice Birds are separate mutations which occurred in captive breedings. All are domestically raised and do not occur in the wild state. Neither are expensive in this country.

The latter two color varieties and domestically raised Gray Rice Birds are excellent breeders, but wild trapped Grays show little inclination to breed in captivity. Therefore, domestically raised birds are always a little higher in price than wild trapped birds, but they are always worth the extra cost. No one can look at Gray Java Rice Birds and tell for sure whether or not they were trapped in the wild state or raised in captivity.

Javas nest in a standard Budgerigar nest box with plenty of nesting material. Incubation time is thirteen to fourteen days, and chicks leave the nest in three weeks.

GOLDEN SPARROW

The aggressive Golden Sparrow from Africa must be housed with weavers and other overbearing birds. Though the size is four and a half inches, the body is rather slight because the tail is rather long. It cannot be called a beautiful finch, but it is extremely hardy. It will live on the standard parrakeet or finch diet and likes mealworms, but it can do without them.

The male is attractive with his black beak, bright yellow head, neck, and underparts and warm brown back and wings. The female has a neutralized and colorless shading with dull buffish-yellow on all areas except for the brownish-straw wings. The beak is a pale horn color.

QUAIL FINCHES

The strangest of all finches is the highly fascinating but rarely available Quail Finch which has adopted the markings as well as the terrestrial habitats of quails. The several races show minor variations with lighter or darker shadings. The standard finch diet is required, and small live foods in addition to mealworms are necessary for success in breeding. Concrete floors are unsatisfactory. Food and water must be placed within easy reach of the ground. Dust baths are preferred to liquid bathing.

Quail Finches are shy, spending most of their time hiding in grasses where they also nest most successfully. They seem to dislike perches and open aviaries. If frightened they panic like quails and fly upwards without regard to aviary roofs which may be hazardous.

The coloring of Quail Finches provides protective camouflage. Their subdued colorings of dusky-brownish on the upperparts are enhanced by fine white bars on the dark upper chest and flanks. Adjoining areas are bright chestnut, and the central abdominal area is grayish fading to white in the ventral area. The male has a blackish area covering the forehead, throat, and face. The female shows dusky brown in these areas and a buffish shade in the barred areas. The lower mandible is always reddish, but the upper mandible may vary from red to black. In some races, a bright white underlines the eyes. The size is approximately three and a half inches including the short tail.

CUBAN MELODIOUS

The small, alert, and ever active Cuban Melodious is attractive. Though it has many of the vivacious charms of waxbills, it becomes aggressive, especially during the breeding season, and should be housed with larger, more defensible birds. Not all individuals are bullies; but, if the bird fancier does not maintain a watchful eye, this little Grassquit may soon have all birds plucked.

Three and a half inches in length including the tail, the Cuban Melodious is slightly more plump than most waxbills. Like the African Fire Finch, it spends a great amount of time on the ground hunting for seeds and small insects. In an aviary it is steady and tame, more than reasonably hardy, and seldom fails to attract attention.

It is a good breeder in captivity if it is given insectile mixture and a variety of live foods in addition to the standard finch diet. Both sexes cooperate in incubation and in rearing the children; but, once they are weaned, the youngsters should be removed to prevent harm from parents who wish to go to nest again. One pair per aviary brings greatest breeding success. In the wild state these birds claim certain areas as their own; and, if other Cuban Melodious Finches should intrude, the males fight furiously.

The male Cuban Melodious, which sings happily and often, cannot be called melodious; but he is attractive. Intense black covers the beak, cheeks, lower facial area, and throat. This area is brilliantly framed by a broad circular sweep of yellow starting with a fine yellow line above the eye and widening downwards to include the upper chest area. This is followed on the chest by a less intense shade of black bordering the yellow. The lower chest and abdominal areas are grayish-olive, and upperparts are dull olive-green.

The female has a brown facial area instead of black, and the yellow is greatly reduced. Chest areas are grayish-olive.

CUBAN OLIVE

The Cuban Olive Finch is slightly larger, far more aggressive, less attractive and less popular. It occurs in a much wider range including Mexico and parts of Central America.

The basic colors are the same, but the pattern is arranged in a far less attractive manner. The bright yellow on the male is reduced to prominent but short eyebrows and a small chin patch which dips into a mustache at the corners of the lower mandible. Beak and face are black, and other coloring is like that of the Cuban Melodious.

The female, like the female Cuban Melodious, is dull by comparison. Black is absent, and yellows are greatly reduced. This species prefers to nest rather low in shrubbery if given the chance.

JACARINI FINCH

Another Grassquit extensively native to Cuba, Mexico, Central America, and South America is the Jacarini Finch which is not often available and not highly popular. It has a pleasantly peaceful, even shy disposition. It is not a good breeder.

In appearance, the male resembles the all-black Combassou except for the slender all-black beak and small patches of white on the scapulars and sides of the chest.

The female is very dull and indistinctly marked with brownish upperparts and pale grayish underparts.

BLACK CRESTED FINCH

The Black Crested Finch from South America is sometimes called the Pigmy Cardinal because of the handsome crest. It is somewhat more expensive than the average price for finches, but it is always quickly accepted by the discerning fancier. It is a good breeder provided its live food requirements can be met. Small live foods and an insectile mixture should be provided along with mealworms. Otherwise the standard finch diet is adequate.

Yellow Winged or Red Legged Honeycreepers are excellent aviary birds and are among the easiest of all nectar feeders. The brilliant colors of the male during the nuptial season never fail to attract admirers. The dazzling turquoise cap does not show in this picture, and the legs of the male are usually a brighter reddish shade. The female is actually soft green and not nearly as drab as this picture indicates.

Pekin Nightingales are lovely birds with bright personalities and extremely active natures. They are ideal subjects for beginners of softbilled birds. Their songs can be beautiful especially in uncrowded planted aviaries. The writers do not consider them good cage birds because they are too active. Close quarters cramp their style and remove much of the joy which they otherwise convey quite freely in proper aviaries.

The male has a sharp and very pleasant arrangement of its blacks, whites, and grays. The long, shapely black crest is nearly always erected. The rest of the head is white except for a broad swath of black covering the lores, eyes, and cheek areas. A long, rather narrow black patch also adorns the chin. The rest of the bird is a pleasant and uniform shade of gray which is darker on the upperparts and paler on the underparts.

The female is slightly less bold in color because the blacks and whites are less intense and are shaded with a grayish tinge. The black throat patch is absent. The size is somewhat more than four and a half inches including the rather long tail but excluding the crest.

CRIMSON PILEATED FINCH

Quietly colored and shy, the distinctive and always peaceful Crimson Pileated Finch from South America is costly and not often available. In planted aviaries, which it likes best, this species is likely to hide from view most of the time. In such an aviary, the Crimson Pileated will nest if given the same diet as the Black Crested Finch. Mealworms must be rationed, but they are nevertheless important. Males do not seem as hardy as females for some inexplicable reason.

The male has a flat, almost horizontal crest of bright red hairlike or brushlike feathers bordered on the sides by a dark brownish-black line which, while rather fine, is prominent. This recumbent crest usually lies flat against the crown, but in a show of emotion it is sometimes halfway raised.

All the other coloring in this five-inch species is a quiet brownish with a dull tint of rose which becomes more red and more prominent on the chest and abdomen. The beak is black, and the prominent eye rings are white.

The female is brown with the rose tint absent in all areas except on the rump.

The closely related Pileated or Gray Pileated Finch is the same in every respect except the basic coloring is a soft and quiet gray instead of rose-tinted brown. The crest of the male is bright red, but the female has a chestnut shaded crest. This species is also reasonably rare and somewhat costly.

SAFFRON FINCH

The lustrous and glowing Saffron Finch from South America is a robust and hardy bird of five inches, including its long tail of nearly two inches. It mixes well with Budgerigars, Cockatiels, and weavers; but it is too aggressive to house with small waxbills or Australian finches. It thrives on a parrakeet or finch diet and needs plenty of green foods and fruits. It requires live foods during the nesting season. Saffrons are perhaps overly fond of mealworms; and, since they easily become overweight, both mealworms and oat groats should be rationed except while young are in the nest.

Saffrons are excellent breeders. They prefer the standard Budgerigar nestbox with lots of dried grasses. Males have a vigorous but tuneless and rather harsh song during the nesting season. Incubation time is twelve or thirteen days, and youngsters leave the nest in about two weeks.

The male glows in a bright shade of golden-yellow overlying the entire color scheme. The forehead and crown are rich golden-orange. Upperparts are dark and dusky-greenish with sulphurous-yellow edges on the feathers. The beak is dark horn above and orange-horn below, and the eyes are dark brown. Females are dull by comparison because the yellow underparts are less bright and the golden-orange is absent from the crown.

Immatures are grayish-buff gradually assuming streaks of adult coloring which ultimately takes several months.

WARBLING FINCHES

Only a few of the various Warbling Finches have been kept in captivity in this country, and even these are seldom available. They are good sized and aggressive birds which are safest when housed with weavers and Java Rice Birds. They will accept either a parrakeet or finch diet but should also have fruits, mealworms, and insectile mix during the breeding season.

The extremely hardy and happy Lined or Ringed Warbling Finch reminds one of the Black Crested Finch in general coloring and pattern, but it lacks the beautiful crest and the long slender chin patch. The broad flare of white on the throat is bordered by a large blackish area on the chest. The long tapering white eyebrows, a small white area underlining the eye, and a touch of chestnut on the undertail coverts are noticeable accents. The body coloring of gray is smooth and pleasant. The size is slightly more than four and a half inches in length including the rather long tail.

The Chestnut and Black or Chestnut Breasted Warbling Finch has slate-gray upperparts with a trace of green. A stripe of creamy-white extends above and below the eye. Chestnut-brown covers the chest and sides interrupted by an inverted "V" of white dividing the central abdominal area.

The Pretty Warbling Finch is not an attractive bird. Underparts are buffish-cinnamon or light chestnut, darker in the male and paler on the female. Upperparts are a dark mixture of gray and brown with whitish bars on the wings and a white stripe through the eyes.

SEEDEATERS

The South American Seedeaters are good loud singers, but they are not pretty. The writers have always called them "Miniature Grosbeaks" because of the thick beaks and stout bodies. None are large, but most are aggressive and should be kept with weavers, Cutthroats, and Java Rice Birds. These birds are not often available and only a comparatively few fanciers are familiar with them. They thrive on the same care as given the Warbling Finches and prefer cup-shaped nests for breeding. Females and immatures for most species are dull olive-brown, slightly paler on the underparts. The beaks are blackish.

The White Collared Seedeater is perhaps the best known member of the group. The four inch size includes a tail of nearly one and a half inches. The large beak of the male is yellowish-horn, and the black head is contrasted by a large white area flaring from the chin and forming a collar on the throat which stretches backwards to the nape. A broad black band extends across the upper chest, and the rest of the underparts are grayish-white. Upperparts are grayish with a tinge of brown on the wings and tail. A small white patch marks the base of the primary flight feathers.

The Bluish Finch, slightly smaller, has more grayish-blue than black on the head. The chin is black with fine black lines flaring out to the sides. The black chest band is a little higher on this species, and the yellow beak is more slender.

The Lined Seedeater is similar to the Bluish Finch, but the beak is blackish, and a white line runs down the center of the head. Chin and throat are black, and a large white patch extends across the lower cheek area.

The Variable Seedeater, often called Hick's Seedeater or Lineated Finch, comes from Mexico and Central America and is less than four inches long. Upperparts are black, and underparts are mostly white with gray shadings at the sides. The rump and a small wing patch are white. A broad black band crosses the chest, and a white collar is narrow on the throat and broader on the sides of the neck. The chin is black.

There are two races of Strawberry Finches (*Amandava amandava*). The Indian subspecies is the most common and the least costly. It is usually called Tiger Finch in India. The Oriental or Chinese Strawberry Finch is a brighter red and slightly smaller. This member of the Waxbill family undergoes a seasonal change of color. During the eclipse period the bright male resembles the female which is also pictured here. Photo by Harry V. Lacey.

The Virginian Cardinal, such as the male pictured, available to European fanciers is the Mexican race. Birds of the United States cannot be exported to other countries, nor can they be kept in captivity by American fanciers. Photo by Harry V. Lacey.

Chapter XIII

INTRODUCTION TO POPULAR SOFTBILLS

Several inexpensive and frequently available softbills are so delightful in personality and appearance that it is difficult to resist them. Though their diet is completely different from finches, they are still easy to accommodate. They are called softbills because their diets are composed of soft foods rather than hard seeds. Commercial diets are now available to simplify the feeding task which was once considered ponderous and messy.

The birds selected for this chapter are among the easiest and inexpensive to obtain in softbill groups, and they require simple care. Moreover, they are hardy, and all have a rewarding talent which amply repays the bird fancier in pleasure and amusement.

The simple diet revolves around mynah pellets or mynah meal which is a complete diet for many softbills. Mynahs, by the way, are softbills, too. In all probability, the store where you bought your softbills has already transferred imported birds onto the simplified mynah pellets. In addition to mynah food, the writers offer some fresh fruits (soaked raisins, red apple, and orange), peanut butter, live mealworms, and sometimes nectar. The nectar for the average softbill is simply one part of honey to five parts of water. All these items are relished by the birds, but they must not be fed too abundantly or else the birds might give up the balanced mynah food. Grit is not used for these birds unless they also eat seeds.

Softbills are as a rule extremely lively and are happier in aviaries or large cages. Small cages are too confining and too quickly soiled. Only one of the birds covered in this chapter should be housed with small waxbills or other small finches. Most are all right with larger finches, and most are ideal with cardinals.

PEKIN NIGHTINGALE

The rewarding charms of the Pekin Nightingale are cheerful songs, lively and curious personalities, and a beautiful appearance. This is the least expensive of all softbills and is always the most popular. It is one of the easiest to breed in captivity provided great quantities of live foods are available. It also likes nectar. The nest is small and cup shaped and usually placed low in shrubbery near running water so the parents can bathe frequently.

Sexes are similar, and the size is five inches including a two inch tail. The beak is bright red on the outer half and dull brownish-black on the basal half. The head is dark olive shading gradually into a grayish-olive shade over most of the upperparts. The outer fineline webs of the primary flight feathers are edged in bright yellow with a deep rust-orange shade on about one-third of the inner length. When the wings are folded, this is an attractive and prominent feature. The underparts are dominated by a broad fan-shaped flare of bright yellow starting on the chin and covering the throat. The lower part of this yellow is a deep rust-orange. Remaining underparts are pale olive.

The Shama Thrush is one of the aristocrats among softbilled birds. The rich and melodious song is one of the finest in all the bird world.

The female has a paler shade of red on the beak and less of a flare to the throat. In some cases the yellow is paler, but this is not reliable because there is some fading in captivity.

JAPANESE TUMBLER

The acrobatic genius of the bird world is the amazingly intelligent Japanese Tumbler or Bucket Bird which is a member of the Tit family. Its astonishing gyrations and swift flight in an aviary are matched by frequent somersaults in a cage.

In fact, the moderately priced Bucket Bird is one of the few birds in the world which has its own specially designed cage. Usually made in the orient of bamboo, this cage is tall and rectangular with a balcony. Beneath the balcony hangs a little bamboo bucket dangling on a string. The intelligent Tumbler quickly learns to pull the string when a mealworm is placed in the bucket. The balcony also serves as a springboard for backward somersaults to the perch below.

Tumblers require the standard softbilled diet described above. They also need parrakeet mix, sunflower seeds, and health grit. They emulate woodpeckers in hammering open the sunflower seeds.

The subdued colors and pattern of Japanese Tumblers are not their main charm. The personality is most important with these birds. Sexes are alike. The size is four and a half inches long including a tail of one and three-fourths inches. The sturdy and bluntly pointed black beak is three-eighths of an inch long.

Brazilian Crested Cardinals are too large to be included with most small finches; but they do well with large, strong finches and a great variety of small and medium softbills. In a spacious planted aviary they sing quite freely and melodiously, but in average aviaries they are seldom inclined to sing.

The Shama Thrush *(Copsychus malabaricus)* is one of the finest of all softbilled birds, and if properly fed is a superb songster. There are seventeen subspecies ranging from Ceylon and India throughout Southeast Asia. Those available to aviculturists are from India and Thailand. The race from Thailand has a longer tail and is perhaps a little more handsome. The female, in contrast to the male pictured here, has a drab and soft brown instead of the lustrous shades of black and chestnut. Photo by Harry V. Lacey.

One of the most popular of softbilled birds is the Pekin Nightingale. A simple diet keeps this bird in excellent health.

Pale tan encircles the crown, covers the lores but excludes the eyes, and flares backwards to include the cheeks, and tapers off at the lower end of the neck. An irregular darker tan stripe down the center of the neck starts at the back of the crown and widens till it stops abruptly at the lower end of the neck. The rest of the head is black including a broadly flaring throat patch which also covers the forepart of the chest. The eyes are big and black with a mischievous glint.

The mantle is brown, and the rest of the upperparts are gray slightly shaded with brown. Underparts are mostly dusty-tan with the darker and richer brown of the sides nearly meeting in the center of the chest.

BULBULS

Red Eared and Red Vented Bulbuls from India are frequently available. They are comparatively inexpensive, hardy, and have pleasant songs. The care is the simplified softbill diet outlined at the beginning of this chapter.

The Red Eared Bulbul has a jaunty crest and bright red ear patches. Upperparts are brown, and underparts are white. A thin brown line offers an unusual accent by encircling a large white area on the lower face and cheeks. The size is about six and a half inches including a tail of two and a half inches.

The Red Vented Bulbul has a luxurious crest, a robust shape, and a long tail. It is slightly larger than the Red Eared Bulbul and is overall very dark blackish-brown with pale margins on the feathers of the back, wings, and chest. The brightest note is a large rosette of curly red feathers surrounding the ventral area.

GOLD FRONTED CHLOROPSIS

The enchanting and bright green Gold Fronted Chloropsis is one of the most highly recommended of all softbills because of its fine song, great beauty, and tame personality; but it is somewhat expensive. This seven inch Fruitsucker or Leaf Bird, as it is often called, requires nectar in addition to the softbill diet. The long slender black beak is curved. The facial and throat areas are black. A bright blue divided beard adds a bright accent, and a bright halo of golden-orange surrounds the black area showing noticeably richer in the lower area and very prominently on the forehead and crown. The rest of the coloring is bright, glossy green except for a turquoise shoulder patch.

WHITE EYES

A small and inexpensive nectar feeder ideal for beginners is the charming White Eye or Zosterops. This little two and a half inch sprite is all dull olive-green, paler and somewhat yellowish on the chest and throat. The eyes are surrounded in a bright white ring. The male has slightly more yellow than the female.

Zosterops thrive on nectar food plus fruit, sponge cake, peanut butter, live foods, and mynah meal or mynah pellets. The nectar should contain a small percentage of canned milk, or a dish of dry soya powder should be added along-side the nectar. These birds are adept at hawking small insects in flight.

It is difficult to pinpoint the charm of this species. It is not colorful. It does not sing. Ordinarily it does not become tame, but the charm is there never-theless. People always linger alongside any aviary containing White Eyes. Admiring smiles are greeted by the probing, curious stares of tiny alert eyes spectacled in white. Spectators on both sides of the wire seem reluctant to part company.

TROUPIAL

The big, bold, and bright Troupial is a favorite caged pet in many parts of the world and is usually called the Bugle Bird because it can be taught to whistle bugle calls and tunes. It thrives on the standard softbill diet but likes some extra raw meat and perhaps more live foods than other softbills so far covered in this chapter. Because it belongs to the Hangnest family of New World Orioles, it also appreciates nectar.

The Troupial is an aggressive bird with a sharp beak. Black covers the head, neck, and throat feathers. The lower boundary of black extending onto the upper chest is irregular and jagged. Bare bluish-gray skin surrounds the eyes and tapers to a point behind. Wings and tail are black except for an irregular and broad bar of white slashing across the scapulars into the secondary flights. Remaining plumage is bright golden-orange in the wild state fading into brilliant yellow in captivity.

TOUCANS

There are many species of exotic big-billed toucans and toucanettes which are intriguing and charming pets. Space prevents coverage of the patterns and colors of the different species. Some become very tame. Cuvier's and Sulphur Breasted Toucans are favorites for pets and are readily available at com-paratively reasonable prices. The handsome, comic Toco Toucan is the best pet potential, but it is rare and quite expensive.

The Dusky Twinspot (*Euschistospiza cinereovinacea*) from Angola is very rare in aviculture and is not as attractive as most Twinspots. Upper parts not shown in this picture are slate-black. Sexes are very much alike. Twinspots are difficult when first imported because they will usually not accept a well rounded diet which includes insectile or softbilled foods as well as live foods and seeds. This species is closely related to Dybowski's Twinspot.

The Black Backed or Golden Bellied Grosbeak (*Pheucticus aureoventris*) ranges from Colombia to Argentina. Most Grosbeaks which are available to aviculturists are not very popular. Though pleasant in many ways and easily maintained, few are as attractive as the majority of birds which bird fanciers favor even though some are very pleasant songsters.

Button Quails are excellent additions to an aviary and are delightful birds. The female, center, is less colorful than the male.

Toucans are great comedians and are easily kept in fine condition by a sensible diet using mynah pellets as a basis. This excellent food is a complete diet in itself; but the writers add raw meat, mealworms, diced fruits, and soaked raisins because the birds like these items and because they are very nourishing. The amounts are all limited so that the birds will not desert their basic mynah pellets.

We have covered only a very few of the versatile and unusual softbilled birds. There are countless more with all sorts of color combinations and with or without frills and ornamentations. The most diverse tastes can be satisfied easily in this vast family. For further information on these groups, you will find extensive coverage in *Finches and Softbilled Birds*.